THE ECK-VIDYA

ANCIENT SCIENCE of PROPHECY

PAUL TWITCHELL

D1075846

THE ECK-VIDYA, ANCIENT SCIENCE OF PROPHECY

Copyright © 1972 by ECKANKAR
ISBN: 0-914766-89-9

All rights reserved. No part of this book may be reproduced, stored in a retrieval system or transmitted in any form by an electronic, mechanical, photocopying, recording means or otherwise without written permission of the copyright holder.
Printed in U.S.A.

ECKANKAR, ECK and 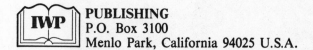 are trademarks of ECKANKAR.

Library of Congress Catalog Card Number: 75-306773

Sixth Printing 1982

IWP PUBLISHING
P.O. Box 3100
Menlo Park, California 94025 U.S.A.

TABLE OF CONTENTS

CHAPTER 1

AN INTRODUCTION TO THE ECK-VIDYA

Those who enter into ECKANKAR, the Ancient Science of Soul Travel must have their roots firmly established in the principles of this particular path to God. Not only in this life must they have these roots well grounded but from the past, the incarnations where cause was created to bring each Soul to this particular spiritual level of unfoldment today where he will be accepted by the Mahanta, the living ECK Master, in this incarnation.

Because of this one always finds the ECK-Vidya different, a bit foreign to his acceptance level, but at the same time refreshing and stimulating. It gives things to the reader and participant of past, present and future that other prophecy systems often overlook. It gives man much to think about, that he has a way to receive and give certain knowledge about one's self which is useful and valuable.

Life is largely a struggle in which man employs the known in an effort to conquer the unknown. Everywhere people are endeavoring to predict the future for meeting it in a more prepared manner. The whole story of the ECK-Vidya is the penetration into the realms of the generally unknown areas, not yet explored by the psychics, scientists, mystics or saints.

The ECK-Vidya discloses there is an abstract design behind all life. Scientists have brought out that there is a science of government material and matter surrounding man. The ECK-Vidya goes further than this, it is the science that shows one how he can govern the visible life by knowing what is going to take place in the future. It is the true science of the prediction of life causes.

The ECK-Vidya involves the principle of the cycles of life. Although some systems of prophecy base their science on this principle it is not greatly understood. Everything in time, in the life of the individual here on this planet and other planets is divided by seven parts. Every seven years we end a cycle and start a new one, but within these seven year cycles we have minor cycles that runs in sevens, and these are divided from years to months, to days, to hours, and to minutes. On the seventh of each named we have a definite change in our lives for better or worse.

It is up to the individual to learn these subtle changes and to make the adjustment as they arise. The minor changes always affect the greater changes. So when one is able to recognize and handle the very smaller cycles within himself, then he is able to bring about control over his life in the inner which controls his whole universe, that which he carries with himself at all times.

Prophecy is the oldest of the mantic sciences in the world today. It has been accepted by billions of people from the dawn of time as authentic and a way for the foretelling of the future. People have depended upon prophecy through telepathy, spiritual mediums, clairvoyants, astrology and oracles.

Few people outside of ECKANKAR have ever heard of the ECK-Vidya, the ancient science of prophecy, which is the modus operandi for delving into the past, present and future, used by the adepts of the Ancient Order of Vairagi—this is the order of the ECK Masters.

The ECK-Vidya is much more inclusive than astrology, or any of the mystical arts which are utilized by the well known ancients and modern prophets of psychic precognition. It uses more Siddhi* powers than the practictioners of prognosis ever dreamed could be possible.

The ECK-Vidya is only an aspect of ECKANKAR, the Ancient Science of Soul Travel, which is the fulfillment of total awareness with the SUGMAD. Prophecy or foreseeing events before they happen, and the Deja-Vu for seeing what has already happened, are on a far greater panorama of esoteric background than any other system of prophecy which are given from the psychic plane levels.

The ECK-Vidya practitioner has the foreknowingness of the deeper and more subtle events of life, even to the all-inclusive

*Spiritual powers.

6

prophecy of a minute by minute mental and physical action which could take place in the individual's worldly life.

ECKANKAR, of itself, is the highest path to God. But in its own broad and comprehensive aspects are included thirty or more facets of spiritual works, such as prophecy, healing, self-realization, the deja-vu powers, siddhi knowledge, omnipresence, making events happen for one's own future, to name a few. All these are carried on upon a higher spiritual level than those of the occult, metaphysical and religious teachings. The vibrations of anyone practicing the ECK-Vidya are so high that those on the lower psychic scale can never be compared with them.

The ancient mystery cults were established on the keystone of prediction. The Elysian, Orphic, Pythagorian, Dionysian and many other ancient mystery schools had initiations which consisted of the chief priest going into trance and giving predictions for those receiving initiation into their respective cults. Most of the works with which members of a mystery school were concerned were based on predictions of some basis or other.

The foundation of the argument against Socrates during his trial was that he was giving the youth of Athens false hopes by predicting the political and spiritual freedom of those who listened to him in the famed Grecian Temples of ancient times.

The most famous of all mystery cults in ancient times was the Oracle of Delphi in the Temple of Apollo at Delphi. Once during a visit to this famous oracle, which is now one of the great tourist sights of ancient Greece, I met an elderly man who made a sudden appearance as if out of thin air, who claimed the Oracle still speaks to those who have the gifts of prophecy and divine insight.

At first his words were taken lightly until while sitting alone at dusk on a great pile of ruins near what was the mouth of the Oracle of Delphi, its words came slowly and distinctly. After the first shock of surprise and recognition that it was not a human voice speaking, I slowly began to understand what was being said.

Frankly, I rose and looked about to learn who was playing pranks, but found no one within the vicinity. The gates to the Oracle grounds had been closed and I had slipped in without detection thinking that at anytime a guard would appear to order me out.

A gentle breeze rustled the leaves of a tree nearby, but to me, through this rustling, a deep voice spoke. "Beloved one, who in these times has been given wisdom to know and understand the gods are immortal, and still have power to grant those willing to listen the power of prophecy and wisdom, you will know and understand the future, past and present of all beings and things. This gift has been given you now."

I knew in a flash that it was the voice of Apollo, the divine god of Greece, whose temple ruins I now stood upon. Standing between the high Grecian columns which were still erect, stark against the glowing sunset sky, I could look down the narrow valley between the sharp mountains to the Ionian Sea, but saw nothing for the words had filled my mind.

I slowly digested what had been spoken. It became apparent that the ancient gods of Greece still lived for those who had ears with which to listen. Shortly afterwards I began the practice of the ECK-Vidya.

Another Oracle of the ancient Greeks was located on the Island of Delos. It was the Oracle of Dionysus, and was one of the great places for prophecy in the ancient world. This Oracle for the gods of Greece was active until about the first century B.C. I visited here several times before it was in the terrible state of ruins as it is now. I found somewhat the same phenomenon occurring as that at the Temple of Apollo at Delphi. It was an exhilarating but awesome experience.

However the Oracle which was still in existence until the first of this century was hidden deeply in the wild mountain ranges of northern Tibet. It was known as the Voice of Tirmer. Named after one of the earlier ECK Masters in ECKANKAR, who was martyred under Shipue, supposedly the first king of Tibet, several hundred centuries B.C., it remained in order until the beginning of this present century. Used less and less by those who knew of its existence it finally faded out when the beings who spoke through it left.

I visited this Oracle twice with Rebazar Tarzs. The first time I was initiated into the Ancient Order of the Vairagi, which is that order of the ECK adepts. The next time to confirm some of the prophecies of my mission in this life, the first being at the time of my birth by an old Cherokee who told my mother that she was to give birth to the emissary of the new world message called ECKANKAR.

The Oracle was one of the oldest on this planet and was used until about seventy years ago by the ECK Masters when initiating chelas into the Ancient Order of the Vairagi.

Very few use the hoary modus operandi of giving prophecy for those who wish to know their future via the ECK-Vidya method. Those ECK Masters who were able to use the ECK-Vidya way of looking into the future have dwindled to a handful, headed by Fubbi Quantz, the abbot of the Katsupari Monastery near the old site of the Voice of Tirmer.

People who are interested do have the ECK-Vidya readings, but anyone who wants to learn anything about this method of prophecy must expect a long, arduous apprenticeship under the Mahanta, the living ECK Master. He must follow the words and instructions to the letter.

The knowledge of the ECK-Vidya and its means of prophecy is not easy. The chela places himself under the tutelage of the ECK Master and awaits instruction on the path of ECKANKAR. It might take him weeks, years and ages before reaching the unfoldment of his spiritual self in order to begin looking correctly at the auras and the lives of others.

By constant practice of the spiritual exercises of ECK, coupled with strong spiritual shocks, the chela is able to awaken the Tisra Til (the spiritual eye) and bring about a release of the Atma Sarup, the Soul body, from the physical putting it above the realms of time and space.

This takes the Atma Sarup upward and through other planes until it reaches the culminating experience of Moksha or Samadhi, that which we know in the west as cosmic consciousness, but known in the circles of the ECK Adepts as the ECKshar.

When Soul is in this position one knows all the future, past and present for himself and others if he should desire.

One does not generally induce the trance state to leave the body, but can do so by what is known among the ECK Adepts as the Saguna Sati. We know it as instant projection, the ability to move out of the physical body, at will, into any of the higher states of consciousness.

I can do this, one way, simply by concentrating on a physical or mental object for a few moments while repeating the secret name of God. There is usually a sound similar to a ping in the right ear. At times however it sounds as loud as a mortar gun. I find myself hovering above the area we know as time and space looking at the records of whomever have asked for a reading of their past, present or future.

What follows is most unusual for so many times while in this position Soul can transfer the knowledge of the records to the physical senses which are active and can use the body for getting this knowledge on paper or tape. After this it means the checking and double checking to see if the facts are right.

The method of doing this is simple but there is a complexity about it which often creates a problem. One does not use the human intellect in this but that part of himself which is beyond the intelligence. In this position the reader sees the lives of the requestee stretched out before him like a deck of cards spread out in a fan shape on the table before him.

What he reads in these cards is entirely up to him. The many lives which one has spent on earth may or may not have anything to do with the present life. But this is up to the ECK-Vidya reader to gather the knowledge needed and report what he thinks are the principal and important lives in which the karmic conditions were created and developed that shows up in the life of the readee today.

For this very reason no two readers will report the same thing. This is why many people cannot understand why one reader says one thing and another something else. It depends upon what the reader thinks best to report, and whether this is correct or not in the determination of the reading as a whole. It is the judgement of the reader to select what is most important to the requestee to help him here and now in this life.

The ECK-Vidya actually means total knowledge. All that comes to him who can read the spiritual records of the Atma Sarup (Soul body), is that which is known as divine.

The practice of the ECK-Vidya has nothing to do with the practice of yoga, spiritualism, drugs, Vedanta, astrology or any kind of rituals. It is not concerned with the asanas (postures), mantrams (chants and vibrations), mudras (gestures and binds), and pranayama (breathing exercises).

Neither does it have any relationship with the intellectual studies in religion and philosophy. It is a field all to its own in an individuality that is immediately recognized when one enters into it.

The ability to give the ECK-Vidya readings depends on the

individual who can do Soul Travel. Here we are dealing with Soul records and not the Akashic. We find the term Akashic records is very popular and a number of people can do this who are able to read these records of the astral planes sufficiently for those who desire to know something about their past lives in this physical world.

But the Soul records consist of past incarnations on the physical, astral, causal, mental, etheric and Soul planes. Anyone who is able to do the ECK-Vidya readings can bring to light any lives which the requestee has spent on any of these planes and what his future might be not only on the physical plane but anywhere in the universes, including the planets of this material world.

The ECK-Vidya works on the principle that the world is interlocking and is a unity which can be observed once we lift ourselves above the regions of time and space. Within this position we are able to see all as a totality and to sort out the powerful magnetic fields around those whom we are reading.

One can be in the midst of a group of people, a crowd, or with only a few friends or relatives and still put himself into the state of higher consciousness. The physical body will continue to function, and he can be sociable and working but still read from this position above time and space.

I have been in the homes of several foreign government officials over the world and talked with them about the affairs of their respective nations, to give them predictions of what the future might hold for them. During a visit to London one summer I was invited to the home of one of the British Ministers. Knowing my ability to use the ECK-Vidya, this official asked several confidential questions about the future of the foreign affairs of his nation. I told him about the troubles Britain would have with China, the economy shift the Prime Minister would make in dropping several cabinet posts and the trouble with the British pound. All of which came true.

However, the goal of ECKANKAR is not to develop the acquisition of Siddhis or supernormal powers of this nature. The ECK-Vidya is only an aspect of the enormous path of ECK to God.

Generally speaking, the ECK-Vidya is the achievement of the spiritual insight with which to look into one's future on a minute to minute basis or day by day reading. It is just another part of the overall aspects of ECKANKAR.

One should never be sidetracked from the ultimate realization with the SUGMAD (God). Our values change as our recognition of the inner strength and relationship with God grows.

This brings us to the point that an ECK-Vidya reading of the Soul records is the highest that anyone can receive for their own benefit. A person who has the ability to do Soul Travel on his own has the talent to read the Atma (Soul) archives and give the ECK-Vidya readings. This type of reading is far more revealing for those seeking to know something about themselves and their future than any other type of readings.

During the first few times in my meetings with Rebazar Tarzs, the great ECK Master, it was possible to learn to read my own records from Soul body. One day while sitting on the side of a steep mountain slope in the Himalayas discussing ECKANKAR, the Ancient Science of Soul Travel, I asked if he would show how the technique of the ECK-Vidya reading was accomplished.

We both projected out the physical body into that world called the Fifth plane (the Atma Lok) where standing beside me in the Atma Sarup, Soul body, Rebazar Tarzs pointed out the millions of my past lives. They looked like a fan of playing cards spread over a table, and were around me like an arc of pictures.

These Soul embodiments of past lives and the future in this life resembled tiny file cards. Each life has a series of pictures, beginning at birth and passing through all events to death, on whatever plane it has embodied itself. We find perhaps several million of these tiny pictures of past lives existing in each Soul; each with a series on every individual life that we have spent somewhere on some plane within the lower worlds, e.g., physical, astral, causal, mental, etheric and Soul planes.

The great ECK Master proceeded to show me the individual lives which I had spent on all the planes in the lower worlds. All these lives were viewed and examined with scrutiny. We were able to look over all the lives needed to be analyzed at the time from this lofty position. We were in the field of total awareness and able to retain a knowledge of what these pictures represented in my long existence in the lower worlds, without looking, as we must do in the lower or psychic planes where matter, energy, space and time must be taken into consideration.

From this position beyond space and time we can see what is in store for ourselves in the future and how to meet it, or how to avoid it. Regardless of what most readers will tell you few if any hardly reach the state of spiritual unfoldment to be able to know and understand such knowledge. Also most readers are psychics and are only reading from the lower planes for the earth incarnations and usually do not have the background material to finish and evaluate for the requestee.

There is another point to consider, no astrologer can take a position of this nature, for he hardly ever has the spiritual unfoldment to get into the worlds beyond space and time. He reads only from a materialistic viewpoint of what is told him via the heavens and stars. This is all that he can give, and never is he able to advise the client what to do. He can only show this is the map of the road ahead for you, and you can take it or not. He never reads past incarnations nor is able to do hardly any advising on spiritual matters which might concern the individual who is getting a reading from him.

Almost anyone who has become proficient at Soul Travel can reach the records of those who request readings of this nature. He bypasses the aberrations of the reader to reach the high consciousness and give all that is possible to whom he is reading. However, it must be remembered that since these records must be transferred into the physical language via the physical senses that human limitations may establish barriers. The readings will have a certain amount of constriction when given and it should be considered in this light.

I have many case histories of the ECK-Vidya readings on individuals in my files, plus the cases of persons whose desire has been to know their incarnations on the other planets in this universe. Each was carefully traced out for him showing the various lives he spent on these planets before moving to the earth world. It was shown how he moved from planet to planet during his many lives. In one case I have shown how one person was the member of a superior order of beings who traveled in space ships and in the Atma Sarup (Soul body).

Another case history was the story of Soul's records of a person's lives on the astral plane between his physical incarnations. It is not a difficult task to read these lives on any particular plane once anyone has caught the knack of Soul Travel. This isn't astral projection, as I have said before but much different from this phenomenon.

There are the ECK-Vidya readings, particularly one whose

13

records I read for him and predicted his future, almost minute by minute for two months, but wouldn't go any further than this because of a lack of time and space in making up such a report. The cost in doing such a reading is too prohibitive, and it's much better for the requestee to receive a general outline of his future for one ahead instead of going into such detail.

For example I had a woman whom I said would have an automobile accident if she went into the downtown area of her city, during a given period. But she took no chances and stayed home for one whole year, not putting her foot beyond the boundary of her yard. This was not the purpose of the reading. I was only warning her what could happen provided that she did not keep her eyes open and her senses aware of what might happen. I only laid down a road map, not a dogma of law.

We make no attempt to discuss or assist in anyone's problems unless asked to do so, for according to the spiritual law, the individual consciousness of a person is his home, and we cannot enter unless invited.

The reader of the Soul records always practices Vairag, the detachment of himself from the emotional and mental states of those for whom he is investigating these records. Under no circumstances can he become involved in the problems of others except to assist them.

So many people write and state that their purpose for gaining the higher consciousness and learning to read the records for others is to help people. This is a negative approach and should rightly be considered as so, but few persons know and understand this point of view because they believe that it is their mission of God on earth to help others. This is particularly true of those who are unable to help themselves.

Frankly, the SUGMAD (God) of ITSELF does not particularly care about the embodiment of men on earth. All IT is interested in is the survival of Soul through Its spiritual unfoldment. When someone speaks to me about wanting to help others, I shy away because this means to do something for a person on a physical basis. This is good intentions, but the actual true purpose of why we are here is to get the spiritual experiences in life so that we can return to the SUGMAD to become a co-worker with IT. This is our only purpose and wanting to heal someone and help them in a problem may not at all be giving that person assistance in any spiritual direction or unfoldment.

Soul records are the most important part of any individual, for all his life files are kept here on the Soul plane, not, as believed in the lower plane bodies. The respective records of lives spent in the various planes are established on each plane, but the collective records altogether are on the Soul plane. One reader may read off the physical or astral plane, another off the causal and mental, but it's usually an ECK-Vidya reader who can do readings off the Soul plane.

It is true of many planes that we live upon are not registered during our human existence as memories. But it's an apparently easy task for anyone to read these lives for a person provided he is apt at the ECK-Vidya readings. For example if we are living on the mental plane and reincarnate in the astral instead of the physical, then it is not any more difficult to read these records than any others. It is also possible to read the lives of many who have been out of the physical body for years such as Socrates, Napoleon and other historical figures in human history. But it does not matter whether they are great or not, even the lowliest peasant can be read through the ECK-Vidya out of any century in the past.

If one who can do ECKANKAR, the Ancient Science of Soul Travel well, then he can station himself in the Atma Sarup (Soul body) on the Fifth plane and can see the past, present and future of another provided he is given permission. He can do this at his own volition if necessary. But he does have to have permission in order to read another.

If he doesn't get this permission and looks at the records of another person without being requested to do so, then he has violated the spiritual law. No reader can take it upon himself to read another unless he is permitted to do so. This is different from reading auras where the reader might see something that endangers the individual and acts accordingly to counter that danger. The aura or field of magnetism around a person and his spiritual records are two different things.

One must remember that the higher he climbs on the spiritual ladder toward the kingdom of heaven, the more will he be granted freedom and the more that he will grant freedom to others, and will give them less interference in their states of consciousness. As we mount the scale toward the SUGMAD the more ethical we become in our state of conduct toward others.

Much misinformation can be given from the lower plane

readings, for we are dealing with maya (illusion) and often make mistakes that are misleading to the reader.

The point which I am making here, is that anyone who has learned to do Soul Travel to any extent can become capable of doing the ECK-Vidya reading method and can read the high records which are stored on the Fifth (Soul) plane and that certain concepts must be made clear before final entry into the higher spiritual worlds.

However, the goal of ECKANKAR is not to develop the acquisition of these Siddhis or supernormal powers of this nature, for the ECK-Vidya is only another aspect of this enormous path to the divine Reality. Generally speaking, the ECK-Vidya is the achievement of spiritual insight with which to look into one's own future on a minute to minute basis or a day by day reading. This is the realization of the great works of the divine Deity in our lives which can be applied to all things and events we meet in the everyday routine of living.

One should never be side-tracked from the ultimate realization with God. Our values change as our recognition of the inner strength and relationship to God occur.

Astrology, reincarnation and karma are the trinity of higher levels of the ECK-Vidya, and definitely has a place within the framework of any reading done from this method. Each of these three aspects, although not important in a sense of being outstanding individually, is taken up and studied in relationship with the ECK-Vidya works. This must be done for Soul must serve in the lower worlds in order to gain spiritual purification, so we are wise in trying to compare these with what the ECK-Vidya gives everyone in the way of gaining knowledge for Soul works in this world.

It says in the Shariyat-Ki-Sugmad (the Way of the Eternal), the holy scripture for those who are following the path of ECK, that we are in this physical universe to gain spiritual experience. The SUGMAD sent us here from out of the heavenly kingdom, the Ocean of Love and Mercy, as untried Souls, to gain spiritual purification. We are like children who must attend school to prepare us for a place in the heavenly worlds.

The lower worlds, which are below the Fifth (Soul) plane, were established as a training school for Soul. It is created in the heavenly world and sent into the lower worlds to receive Its spiritual training and education. Eventually, after many incarnations, Soul is purified by Its experiences, ridding Itself of the lower universal karma, via reincarnations on the Wheel of the Eighty-Four.

The Wheel of the Eighty-Four is the Zodiac, where Soul must spend so many incarnations in each sign, in order to overcome the influences of the Zodiac signs. When It has conquered the Awagawan, which is the Wheel of the Eighty-Four, Soul returns to the heavenly world with the guidance of the Mahanta, the living ECK Master.

After returning to the heavenly kingdom, Soul is able to serve the SUGMAD, as a co-worker in the various planes of the worlds which make up the total universe of the Supreme Deity, because It has gained spiritual judgment and maturity.

It is said that each Soul after leaving the kingdom of the SUGMAD, in the beginning of Its life, will have rounds of births and deaths in the lower worlds, mainly the earth plane. This includes the various and different species of living beings that It must pass through to the human apex, and Its many lives in the form of man and woman.

The eighty-four on the Wheel means the number of times we have births and deaths in the lower worlds. Eighty-four lacs amounts up to eight million, four hundred thousand times, for each lac equals one hundred thousand years. In other words the individual Soul will go through each Zodiac sign seven times in order to be able to conquer the influences outside Itself.

This is true but there is the accelerated way of getting through this karma so that one does not have to spend his time in a round of births and deaths. This way is the path of ECKANKAR which leads to the Ultimate Consciousness of the SUGMAD. However, the influences as reported by astrology exert tremendous pressure on each Soul, unless Soul knows how to handle them, as long as It is using a physical body. Much of the karma that man is working out is that which is natural in any given sign of the Zodiac. As quickly as one learns to overcome the influences of one sign he moves into the next. This may be done anywhere, whether on the earth planet, or any of the other planets.

Following this, Soul moves on to the next plane, after finishing out Its round of incarnations on the physical plane, i.e., the astral, where It will go through a different process until It has reached the end of Its period there. After this, It spends time in the causal plane and then goes on when finished to the mind plane. When It is through with all these, It enters again into the heavenly worlds as a pure, spiritual entity to serve the SUGMAD.

This is a long, slow process, but the way can be shortened provided one can find the Mahanta, the living ECK Master, who will give the chela the true teachings and show him how to get off the Wheel of the Eighty-Four and go straight into the heavenly worlds by Soul Travel.

The Mahanta always shows the chela the simpler way of getting into God-Realization, the ultimate state of consciousness, which cuts through all the illusions that the negative forces, known as the Kal force, try to snare us with and hold each within the lower worlds for an indefinite time. It is the purpose of the Kal force to hold any Soul within its realm, which are the lower planes, as long as possible. There is always a struggle between Soul and the Kal forces to hold It back from entering into the heavenly kingdom.

Any teaching which informs us that Soul must spend Its time as allotted for eight million years or more within the lower worlds is not of the truth. Since ECK encompasses all the teachings of religions and philosophies it serves to lift Soul into Self-Realization and later to the true God-Realization where the boundless consciousness of the SUGMAD gives liberation to Soul.

So much is to be given out to the world about ECKANKAR and Its path to the SUGMAD, that it is doubtful that any one person can do it within the span of years he has in the world. The teachings of the Mahanta, the living ECK Master go on in an ever-widening circle, from the physical plane to those beyond until they take in the whole worlds of the SUGMAD, instructing and teaching all regardless of whatever plane they may be upon.

The ECK-Vidya is a part of the teachings of ECKANKAR, and must be studied by every chela who wishes to have the true knowledge of the SUGMAD and ECK.

CHAPTER TWO

THE ECK-VIDYA AS THE OLDEST PROPHECY SYSTEM

The ECK-Vidya is the oldest of all the systems of prophecy. It is that modus operandi of delving into the past, present and future of any person who comes to an ECK-Vidya reader. But it has been used mainly by the adepts of the secret Order of the Vairagi, which is the brotherhood of those great Masters who follow the path of ECKANKAR, the Ancient Science of Soul Travel.

The ECK-Vidya reader is not the same as any that you find giving forecast of the future, or reading fortunes. He is generally a prophet. He is one who conveys divine utterances and serves as a mouthpiece of the SUGMAD. His utterance often foretells the future and warns and announces the inevitable, or replies to clients consulting the oracle. Sometimes it is equated with prediction, but this isn't the same. It is said that prophecy is a matter of telling forth, and prediction is that of foretelling. The prophecy is of course the more prominent of the two.

The ECK prophet differs from the religious functionaries and representatives of religious authority in that he claims no personal part in his divine utterance. He speaks not his own mind from the revelation which arises from within himself, which is given him by the ECK. He is possessed by the ECK, that spiritual power which flows out of the SUGMAD into all the worlds giving life to every living being and creature.

The Mahanta, the living ECK Master, is the prophet for all the works of ECKANKAR. When he gives prophecy it is under the possession and influence of the ECK; it can range from the infuse of the heightened powers to the frenzied ecstasy. It can be spontaneous or induced by a series of techniques, mantras, spiritual exercises of ECK, or directly by Soul Travel.

The prophetic state may be accompanied by visions, auditions, and other experiences as well as by total loss of consciousness. However, very few of any the prophets of the ECK-Vidya have ever worked in this manner. But using the criterion of inspired speech, it has become possible to distinguish the ECK prophet from related types of religious functionaries. Although he acts as the diviner, he is largely dependent upon that divine power known as the ECK, and which he has at his disposal.

The nonprophetic divination uses or manipulates objects as in psychic phenomena, consults the spirits of the dead and sometimes cards, such as the Tarot and regular playing cards. Some make predictions such as ESP and other means of the psychic forces to give their views of a doomed event or to make some person temporarily happy. These are the ordinary soothsayers who put up a stand on the street corners for the selling of their wares which are in a sense rather shoddy, and deals with limited and specific needs of many who are filled with anxieties and woes.

The ECK-Vidya prophet is impelled by the divine forces of the ECK to articulate a message of profound and fundamental importance to his own people but not in a destructive or reforming sense. Since he has always been concerned with the message of the ECK he has never taken up reform, been a sectarian leader or tried to become a religious founder. Such is true of Zoroaster, Muhammed, Buddha and others who have connected with all these aspects of religion as mentioned here.

Many of the Israelite prophets were concerned with criticising their own society and introducing revolutionary ideas in the light of what was believed to be the divine being speaking about the future of the peoples of their nation, or as often as not their enemies. Prophets as a distinct class within the Israelite society first appeared in the days of Samuel and Saul, about the tenth century B.C. The tradition of these uncontrollable spokesmen for the God of Israel occupied an important position within the community, as much as the ECK-Vidya prophet does today within the world community.

The prophetic bands of ECK-Vidya Masters have continued over the centuries having established themselves in the main stream of life in practically every community or nation in the world. Their prophecies have saved many a nation and yet on the other hand the same can be said in the opposite manner. Many have been martyred because of their outspokenness about forthcoming disaster for varied nations. Yet none of these were, as the members of Israelite cultic prophets, uncontrolled in their inspired utterance, visionary experiences and predictions of the future. They were in full control of their senses and spoke with clarity to all concerned.

Several of the ECK Masters suffered, for example Geutan who was the Mahanta, living ECK Master, on the continent of Lemuria, prior to its destruction by earthquakes and the sea, was almost slain for his utterances in public about the behavior of the wealthy and the suppression of the poor. This coupled with his dire warnings of what was going to happen to the world of Lemuria, known generally as Mu, made him a hunted man. He escaped but it was only a few years later that the whole continent went under with the upheaval of land masses by earthquakes, and the vast waves of the ocean rolled over it.

The semantic drama of utterance of the prophets of the various cults and religions has become wide indeed. They have covered ethics, passionate social criticism, injustice of the ruling authorities, defense of the poor and a multitude of other things. Among those noted in history as great prophets are: Zoroaster, the founder of the Parsisism, the Persian-Iranian religion; Muhammed, the founder of the Moslem faith; Savonarola, a Catholic priest reformer of the 15th century in Florence; George Fox, founder of the Quaker religion; Joseph Smith, founder of the Mormon religion; Jacob Boehme, a 17th century German mystic and writer; the Pentecostals and dozens of others too numerous to name here, including the Jewish prophets, Nathan, Elijah, Isaiah, Jermiah to name a few.

Of course there were many among the American Indians such as Tenskwatawa and his brother Tecumseh, leaders of the Shawnee tribe against the U.S. Government troops in 1805-13. Sitting Bull was the prophet of the Sioux tribe who wiped out Custer's Seventh Michigan Cavalry at the Little Big Horn.

All religions and cults whether they were primitive or modern have had the prophet who brings warnings against those violating moral laws, social codes and many other things. They utter warnings about natural phenomena such as earthquakes and floods, etc. They speak from many sources, sometimes divination, magic, shamanism, augury and visionary experiences. Situations of stress have frequently produced leaders showing certain resemblance of the biblical prophets.

The I Ching, a book of the Chinese prophecy gives a method

and way of learning the future and gaining knowledge on others. But astrology works in an altogether different manner, while the ECK-Vidya is completely different from either of these two methods. Its history goes back into the prehistoric times.

The very interesting aspect of the ECK-Vidya is that the Mahanta, the living ECK Master, can see into the past and read the past lives of the individual who makes such a request, or what is going on in the present, and also look into the future years ahead if necessary.

With the use of the ECK-Vidya method I have been able to see and know my own past lives for the past thousands of years having been on this earth plane, or generally see into the future when necessary. Although I lived in the tumultuous times of Jesus, it's possible to look back into that particular life today with a more objective viewpoint and see that he was the victim of a plot, created by the rebels who were trying to overthrow the Roman Government and by his own disciples.

All through history have I lived, but as said, now it's feasible to look into the past and see what really took place. The big lie practiced by Hitler and his Nazi staff was nothing new. Using the ECK-Vidya, I learned that Ramses II who reigned about the twelfth century B.C., attacked the Hittites under Muwatallis, to wipe out that nation at a place called Kadesh. Although he had an overpowering army of twenty thousand troops and the best of weapons, Ramses lost the battle through blunders, and his dream of bringing Hitti into the Egyptian empire. Retreating back into Eygpt he worked out the big lie that he won the battle and left most of his troops in charge of Hitti. He ordered the news of his victory spread throughout the land, written on clay tablets, plastered on walls, and had monuments erected. For three thousand years the world believed what Ramses had said. Furthermore, he was forced into a treaty for boundary between the two nations, but twisted the report of the treaty to his own people saying that he was winner of it. When forced to give his daughter over to the Hitti chief to prove his trustworthiness in the treaty, Ramses even lied about this.

I can go into dozens, and perhaps hundreds, of past lives in the same manner which only gives some idea of what working with the ECK-Vidya means to the person who is getting a reading via this method.

The components of the ECK-Vidya are somewhat similar to the

zodiac in the sense that it has a cycle of twelve periods within the year, although the original cycle had thirteen periods. These periods were shortened to include twelve months, twelve years making one cycle. This means that it takes one hundred and forty-four years to complete a full cycle of man's existence on earth. In antediluvian times this was the length of man's years on this planet.

The Wheel of the ECK-Vidya has twelve spokes, the original sections of time which made up the calendar of all nations that existed before the great flood. In ancient times there were thirty days in each month. In the course of time the present calendar was worked out to include twelve months with a varied number of days. In the ancient times the growing seasons and daylight were precious, so the months were named for rare jewels. Only kings and the very wealthy were able to own jewels and so, royalty was considered the favorite of the gods.

Anyone who uses the ECK-Vidya does not use mechanical standards, as in astrology. There is no chart to be drawn up and one does not think in terms of planetary vibrations. The ECK-Vidya is a method of reading the individual Soul records, which does not depend upon plotting and knowledge of mathematics.

Those Initiates of the Fifth Circle in ECKANKAR, generally known as the Mahdis, can usually do the ECK-Vidya. Naturally only a few will attain this level, but because as said before the ECK-Vidya is one of the thirty-two aspects of ECKANKAR which are developed in learning the spiritual works of ECK. Those few who have learned it are showing spiritual development; but one day they will cease to read publicly as I have done, because of a lack of time or because they have risen above this stage of unfoldment in their advance toward God-Realization. In some cases it is taught to the individual who has reached the state of the Initiation of the Fifth Circle (plane) in ECKANKAR.

There are no sacred numbers in the ECK-Vidya. It has nothing to do with numerology, although we do consider the number twelve to mean something to the ECKist. This is because of the cycle of twelve periods within the year, and the twelve years which make up the cycle in a man's life. But since the ECK-Vidya works only with looking and seeing from the Atma (Fifth) plane, it has nothing to do with either numbers or numerology.

23

The period of the twelve year cycle is very important in the life of those who follow the path of ECKANKAR. It means there is a chemical change in the life of the ECKist every twelfth year. His metabolism slows down so that there is a chemical change in the body for every twelve years. This is the reason for most of the people who follow ECK having a greater longevity than those who do not. The very reason of this is because Soul Travel brings about a different type of change in the body than vegetarianism and other means of trying to gain longer life as through nutrition or yoga exercises.

The spiritual exercises of ECK are beneficial to the body for they work off the karma which is often the reason for early death in many a person. The worries, anxieties and other things which come about are often the results of the karmic pattern of the individual's life. Whether the individual can successfully do what is known as Soul Travel or not, the spiritual exercises of ECK will build up his stamina and give him longevity. If he practices his spiritual exercises for a year it will reduce the speed of his bodily vibrations and give him a longer and more healthy life.

The greatest problem of the living ECK Master is the reducing of the body, mental and spiritual vibrations of the individual. In these modern times with all its stress upon the human self man is lifted in his individual vibrations to increasing them to a point beyond anything ever known in the history of the human race. These vibrations cause body weakness, bring on physical complications, and mental stress. If they are too fast there is likely to be some disease attack the body. By reducing these vibrations then the person is well again.

This can be done by the Mahanta, the living ECK Master. Often he works through one of the Mahdis, his disciples, who are the Initiates of the Fifth Circle. But generally if the Mahdis is closed to the Mahanta, for any particular reason, he is unable to give the necessary reduction of the vibrations for he is not a channel at that particular moment.

The accuracy of the ECK-Vidya with astrology, numerology or any other type of prophecy systems is quite different. Astrology and the ECK-Vidya work in altogether different fields. Astrology is a mechanical force that is the Kal force which is the negative aspect of the universe, which states only the prospects of what could take place. The ECK-Vidya is more accurate for it definitely states the karmic pattern of the individual who is being read that

24

shows him having certain happenings and events in his life.

The ECK-Vidya reader is above the planes of time and space and can see the past and future time track. He does not work with ESP, but with the definite reading of the records of the individual Souls. The Soul embodiments of past lives are similar to tiny file cards; each is a life with a series of these pictures beginning at birth and passing through all events to death, on whatever plane It has embodied Itself. Looking further, the reader can see what is going to happen to the individual in the present life and future lives. Astrology cannot be read any further than a few years ahead in this life. Maybe through a whole life but not into any future lives, and certainly not the past lives of any individual.

This is the most interesting phase of the ECK-Vidya reading which hardly any other type of reading has, that of looking into the past lives of any individual who makes such a request. This means then that the living ECK Master will never read anyone without permission. It is against the spiritual law for him to enter into the consciousness and read a person without permission. Anyone who does this certainly makes a mistake for they are apt to take on the karma of whoever they read and pay for this deed. The consciousness of the individual is his own home, and if he doesn't welcome anyone into it, it is a discourtesy to enter. Too many people are naive about this point, that is they are ignorant of their own selves, and wear their problems, troubles and feelings upon their own sleeves. In doing so they invite anyone to enter their house of consciousness, which is like welcoming a criminal or a murderer into it.

This is why one must be cautious in speaking about his inner thoughts to others such as revealing his experiences in the esoteric worlds, or making known his problems to those who do not have the least of experience in advising or consulting of them.

This brings up the point of past lives again and remembering them again with the ECK-Vidya method. This time I give the example of the plot against Jesus which was witnessed during the tumultuous times of that era in Jerusalem. The betrayal of Jesus by Judas was for a particular reason that was to bring about a revolt which would put a certain group of Jewish rebels in power, over the Romans and population, as well as the priestcraft of the Jewish element in Judea.

The idea of betraying Jesus was to force him into using divine

25

powers to save himself and his followers, an act that would certainly convince the multitudes at the Passover Feast that he was indeed the Messiah and bring them flocking to his side. The rebels had nothing to lose by betraying him to the authorities, for, if he were the Messiah, his power would place them in immediate control. If he were not, the seizure of Jerusalem would enable them to launch a new war to drive the Roman conquerors from their homeland.

However, the high priest Caiaphas had caught the rebels by surprise and seized Jesus in the dead of night, had him sentenced to death by a portion of the Sanhedrin, the Jewish court, sitting together as a rump court. He transferred Jesus to Pontius Pilate, the Roman governor, for the death sentence before the city came awake. To make sure that Pilate would approve the execution he aroused the Temple rabble, mainly the ones who held licenses for their activities at the will of the high priest and paid a considerable amount into the Temple coffers for their privilege, to demand the crucifixion of Jesus.

Caiaphas's fortune laid with the Roman conquerors, and not the rebels. He again broke up another of the many plans with which the Jewish loyal groups had sought to wrestle the control of the Judaean heartland and the city of Jerusalem from Rome. He plotted it so well that he became the favorite of the Roman authorities.

The cycles of the ECK-Vidya which is divided into twelve years is called the Lhokhor. There is also another cycle of years for the ECK-Vidya system known as the Rabjung, which consists of sixty years. The year in which each month is named after certain precious jewels, is followed by the twelve year period in which each year is named after the certain elements of nature. It is used for divination of the individual who has requested a reading for what is called a short term period. The sixty-year cycle is used for generally the natal divination of the individual from birth to grave. Often, as in the old days the reading would run over this period and sometimes include two sixty-year cycles or perhaps three cycles.

Sometimes the child who is given an ECK-Vidya reading at his birth is also advised to wear certain stones, especially that under which month he is born. If it is the Month of the Diamond, he should be given a diamond by his parents shortly after the ECK-Vidya reading, blessed by the Mahanta, the living ECK

Master, and worn on his person for the rest of his life. He may also be given an ECK-amulet which can be kept on his person during his lifetime.

The main purpose of the ECK-Vidya is to give man an understanding of himself. It has always been this since the magical schools of Atlantis, and the mystery cults of ancient Lemuria, where the sacred stream of learning has flowed toward the regions of Africa, Persian Gulf, Chaldea, and ancient Egypt. It was carefully hidden from the profane eyes and given only to those who were able to understand and absorb its wisdoms of teaching. Later astrology came into vogue as the so-called master teachings of divination and pushed the ECK-Vidya aside as it became profitable for the priestcraft to sell horoscopes and geegaws which made the buyer happy, with the idea he could know what his future might be and have protection against evil.

The ECK-Vidya does not imply finality in its reading. On the contrary, probably two-thirds of man's so called misfortunes are the results of his ignorance. Man, when ignorant of the laws of the spiritual worlds which control his existence and destiny, is somewhat like a lifeless log floating with the stream. It may be that the various currents of the river will carry him safely to the river's mouth and launch him uninjured upon the great Ocean of Love and Mercy. But it is more likely that the winding course of the river of life will land him in a sandbar of trouble where he will remain for the balance of his days. It could be that he might be liberated by some stronger current which could float him again into some whirlpool of destruction. Either way he has little chance of salvation until he has taken up the path of ECKANKAR.

Under such a state of bondage the ECK-Vidya tends to release the individual. Knowledge isn't the final answer but it is certainly a step along the way to God in helping relieve human suffering and social inharmony. Love is the real liberator, and it comes in the understanding of what one's life is and can be through the ECK-Vidya.

The ECK-Vidya, in its purity, through forming a system of divination, is totally unconnected with either fortune-telling or sensitive, irresponsible mediumship. It is a divine science of prophecy in which the knowledge and understanding of the past, present and future become blended in a natural, harmonious manner. They begin to work together for the benefit of one's own life and understanding. The ECK-Vidya was being seriously studied among the adepts of the Ancient Order of the Vairagi, as a science, for almost fifty thousand years on earth and it has continued to be studied as such by this small group of ECK Masters. The ECK-Vidya has its entire basis in the scientifically established and accepted fact that there are laws and order in practically every universe in God's worlds, including the heavenly kingdom.

When one refers to the Ziquin of the ECK-Vidya it's meant above the psychic planes. Zi is a word in the Amdo language, the dialect of a community of persons on the northeast border of Tibet and China, which is also the name of a large Chinese province. It is in this region that ECK has been most prominent and well known. Zi means above, and the word quin means five; therefore, Ziquin is that which is above the Fifth plane, the plane from which the ECK-Vidya readings are made.

The word will be used time and again throughout this book. So it is well that the reader will keep it in mind as he studies the ECK-Vidya method.

Two other words are concerned with the ECK-Vidya here. First is the Saguna Sati, which is the name of the method used by the ECK Masters, that is, the instant projection from the physical body to the Fifth plane, be it for reading or to enjoy the bliss of God.

The other word is the Bhavachakra, which is the Wheel of Life, or that which those in ECKANKAR call the cycle of the ECK-Vidya. The Wheel of Life is used by the ECK Masters to utilize divine wisdom as a means of informing the mind of man of the very nature of his existence. In other words, the ECK-Vidya is a method of divination based upon the very ancient understanding of the Samsara (the world of changes which is the psychic universe – the lower planes.)

I have personally long considered the ECK-Vidya to be far in advance of psychology and psychiatry because the latter two deal with the mental traits and behavior of the individual. Although one can take up and study the ECK-Vidya method he can also apply it to the nature of man in the human state and see and understand many things in the individual at this physical level.

However, the main purpose is to provide a penetrating insight and full dimensional understanding of the spiritual sum-total of the characteristics and ways of the individual whether he is on this physical plane or in the highest world of God.

Furthermore, the ECK-Vidya sheds fully explanatory light on the frustrations, the obsessions and compulsions, the anxieties and complexes, on all the mental and emotional problems that so often require extremely lengthy psychoanalysis before they can be identified and resolved. Also the ECK-Vidya reveals the details of the mental, emotional and spiritual activities of the individual. Needless to say, identification of the various causes and their relationships involved in such activities is in itself sufficient to provide a clarification of the deeper troubles bothering the individual.

This brings forth a new light on the ancient truths which have not been given before. It is the secret wisdom passed down through the ages generally orally by the ancient adepts of the Order of the Vairagi. They did not teach many the secret wisdom of the ECK-Vidya, and those who gained it were only the initiates of the ECK Circles, who were in training to become Masters of ECKANKAR. But we do find that they advised the ancient Chaldean kings, the Chinese emperors and the Pharoahs when called upon. They were not prominent but on the other hand no ECK Master ever sought to be known publicly. None could feed the ancient wisdom to the general public, for it was the sole knowledge of the ECK Masters and they knew that it was best to keep such wisdom from the public.

To be a fairly successful and happy person, one must have knowledge of himself, and he must be able to understand the people he meets and with whom he has any interaction. Therefore self-knowledge, or what is commonly known in ECKANKAR as Self-Realization, requires an ability to make accurate, objective inventory and appraisal of one's own personality, the traits, potentials, capabilities, character assets and liabilities with which he has been endowed. Then he is able to make the best of life, of all things which are good and positive, correct or adjust those things which are negative or bad. Thus he is able to set himself on a straight, smooth road to greater achievement, gratification and fulfillment in all areas and activities of his life.

There is one great rule that goes in the ECK-Vidya. "Whosoever, and whatsoever is born or done at a given moment of time has the qualities of that moment of time."

We have to abide by this rule for it gives each of us that opportunity to examine ourselves minutely and gain new, sharp

29

insights into one's own particular nature at all levels of existence. Knowledge of the prevailing qualities at birth or the particular event provides answers to many and usually most previously baffling questions about one's own self, and those within his own environment.

Then once the qualities and influences of the various planes come into focus with the individual, one has an in-depth study which eliminates very little in the individual's spiritual and physical makeup. Whatever problem is bothering that individual will certainly be in the foreground and proper steps are taken to eliminate it through the ECK-Vidya.

A lot of philosophy and background goes into the ECK-Vidya, for example the life cycles of men, nations and planets are important in the readings through this method.

These are important because they are connected with the journey of Soul through all the cycles of time in order to perfect Itself. By the use of measurement we can somewhat compare the months of the modern calendar with that of the ancient ECK measurements of time.

They are as follows: January — the month of the emerald, called Astik in the ECK world, or the days of wisdom. February — the month of the bloodstone, called Uturat, or days of love. March — the month of the jade, called Garvata, or days of joy. April — the month of the opal, called Ebkia, or days of hope. May — the month of the sapphire, called Ralot, or the days of truth. June — the month of the moonstone, called Sahak, or the days of music. July — the month of the ruby, called Kamitoc, or the days of freedom. August — the month of the diamond, called Mokshove, or the days of light. September — the month of the agate, called Dzyani, or the days of friendship. October — the month of the jasper, called Parinama, or the days of beauty. November — the month of the pearl, called Hortar, or the days of wealth. December — the month of the onyx, called Niyamg, or the days of charity.

Men, nations, communities and planets are affected in a sense by higher vibrations which rotate every twelve years and change into a different cycle. Souls make up nations, communities, and inhabit planets as beings and human bodies. Therefore, they are influenced by the twelve year cycle. Each time a twelve cycle passes, a Soul or group of Souls are lifted higher into another level of spiritual unfoldment.

The years within the twelve period cycle have each a name given, the name of some nature. They are first, the Year of the Fierce Winds; Second, the Year of the Bright Snows; Third, the Year of the Brilliant Sun; Fourth, the Year of the Beautiful Flowers; Fifth, the Year of the Full Moon; Sixth, the Year of the Strange Storms; Seventh, the Year of the Wandering Seas; Eighth, the Year of the Bountiful Earth; Ninth, the Year of the Abundant Fruits; Tenth, the Year of the Raging Fires; Eleventh, the Year of the Lavish Grains; and Twelfth, the Year of the Trembling Leaf.

All of these work in harmony with one another, and each become individual years within the cycle. Man can live all twelve years within a single cycle as well as he can in a full period which takes in each individual year. It is well to know these years and cycles for they could play an important part in the ECK-Vidya reading of the individual and the secret wisdom which he comes to know about himself and others. More will be given about them in later chapter.

Nations and civilizations have all ultimately suffered, were destroyed, withered away and with them their science, literature, traditions and knowledge. Even Rome fell, and afterwards Europe and the Middle East were wastelands for many centuries for that long sleep called the Dark Ages. But through these centuries the ECK Masters of the Ancient Order of Vairagi succeeded in preserving their collective and ancient knowledge on ECKANKAR.

Although the teachings had no national identity, they were indeed hidden in such places as the Katsupari Monastery, in northern Tibet, or Agam Des, the spiritual city in the remote Himalayan mountains. They have been preserved by many ECK Masters, but mainly through the efforts of Fubbi Quantz, who is the Abbot of the Katsupari Monastery and many hundreds of years old, or Yaubl Sacabi, heading up the spiritual city of Agam Des, and known to be ancient in age, and of great wisdom.

Such secret knowledge as the Egyptian, ancient Greek and eastern religions and many others became lost. But the ECK wisdom has been kept alive and vital by the adepts of the Vairagi, deeply hidden in the Temples of Golden Wisdom. This has been handed down, growing steadily from one generation to the next, ever since the dawn of time in this world. Included in it is the sum total of the ECK-Vidya which these Masters have amassed in the thousands of years in this plane and the others.

Inevitably, all the secrets of the secret wisdom had to be collected in one form, collated and set down in a permanent form which became the Shariyat-Ki-Sugmad. We find this record of secret wisdom now a holy book divided into approximately twelve books, and each section placed in a Temple of Golden Wisdom in the many planes throughout the universes of God.

In the lower worlds there are seven major Temples of Golden Wisdom: two on Earth, one on Venus, and one successively on the astral, mental, causal and Soul planes. These are gathering places for those who travel consciously or unknowingly during sleep. These fortunate Souls are usually taken by the living ECK Master to one of these fountains of knowledge to gather esoteric wisdom.

Many of the ECK Masters who formerly lived and served their apprenticeship in the lower world have established themselves on the various planes in these ancient temples of wisdom, to teach Souls the ancient wisdom of the Shariyat-Ki-Sugmad, which also includes the ECK-Vidya.

They only work with and teach those who belong to ECKANKAR, because this is what the ancient ECK wisdom is concerned with, in its entirety. The underlying principle of the ECK-Vidya is that the universes of God are not only orderly, but that there is interrelation, indeed, a unity present and operative in all things. The ECK-Vidya holds that there is a correspondence between all, even the greatest and smallest parts of the universes.

For example the ECK-Vidya is not content to evaluate and interpret planetary influences alone. It investigates beyond them into the higher levels of what might be termed interlinked governing forces. Then, of course, it postulates the sharp delineation and individuality of the person within the areas and cycles of time as established by the ancient science of the ECK-Vidya.

Once an in-depth profile of an individual is drawn, it is possible to give constructive counsel and counseling and provide definite guidelines for correcting or eliminating faults and shortcomings in the spiritual sense of the individual. Potentials and the probability of achievement and attainment can be greatly increased. In other words the individual can gain all the insight into himself needed for the control of his daily life and karmic pattern.

There are three parts in which the ECK-Vidya can be taken up as a study. First, is that of the individual and his relationship with the cycles of time, be it monthly or yearly. Secondly, is that which is for nations and people. This part concerns itself with the outlook for countries, even the entire world. It seeks to determine what spiritual and kalistic influences will have the greater effect on the social, political, economic and other trends and development. Third, is that which gives in advance the varied rise and fall of the psychic tides which influence the life of every man and woman within these lower worlds. It can be concerned with weather changes, earthquakes, floods and volcanic eruptions.

As said previously the reading of the individual Soul records is done on the Fifth plane of consciousness. The ECK-Vidya reader must be able to travel to this plane (the first of the true spiritual planes; all below it are in the psychic realm) in the Atma Sarup, the Soul body, to examine the records of that individual for whom he is reading.

The lower planes up to the Soul plane are the physical, astral, causal and mental. The Akashic of a Soul's varied and many lives on Earth are stored on the third plane, the causal plane.

Many persons who have psychic ability can contact this plane and read for themselves or others, although it is only the lower plane records which are being read. The Soul plane records which the ECK-Vidya can contact grants the ultimate reading for those who desire to know the truth about themselves. The ECK-Vidya reader is able to give an account of every past life which the individual Soul has spent in any incarnation on every plane in the lower worlds, including the physical, astral, causal and mental.

Soul will be incarnated on various planes to work off karma. It spends time on these other planes in various incarnations, even after leaving the physical body, unless It's under the guidance of the Mahanta, the living ECK Master. Therefore astrology is only dealing with a single dimension, the physical plane. No astrologer can read the past lives, nor the future lives of anyone.

This does not mean there is any conflict with astrology and the ECK-Vidya, but that astrology does not go far enough in informing the reader. Many of his problems are karmic and come out of past lives, but astrology is not able to pinpoint these problems because they are beyond the planetary influences and worldly vibrations. So the individual who asks for a reading must think in terms of what he wants. Usually he asks for a reading which concerns his future, but often he might go in for an Akashic reading which consists of his past lives in this world. When he gets this type of reading he can expect to learn something about his past lives and the karmic pattern which has existed over the many years and made him what he is today.

The next type of reading is that which is called the Soul reading, which gives him the many lives he has spent on other planes besides the physical. It also gives him the karma accumulated there, and which makes up part of his life today.

Third is the ECK-Vidya reading which is mostly for the future. It can be given for a single year, for many years, or a whole lifetime for the individual. Usually he gets it for a year's time in order to get more individual details, and this should be a guideline for him in his daily affairs.

CHAPTER 3

THE DIFFERENCE BETWEEN ECK-VIDYA AND ASTROLOGY

The ECK-Vidya is that part of the daily life of anyone who is a follower of ECKANKAR in practical usage and history of the human race which had its origin in Asia and from whence it flowed in succeeding waves of emigration to all other parts of the earth. This accounts for the presence among some few peoples of the earth of traces and traditional knowledge of divine wisdom of ECK whereby it isn't present in the vast majority of races. In many cases the belief and knowledge of ECK and ITS aspect the prophecy has been kept under wraps and hidden from the mundane eyes for centuries, sometimes assuming various disguises, but the skilled chela is able to trace back to the original and true source through the Mahanta, the living ECK Master.

On the other hand that which became known as astrology grew in proportion beginning with the early times of the Chaldeans and tribes which inhabited the basin of the Tigris and Euphrates Rivers in the land known to the ancients as Mesopotamia. Even so astrology as the long arm of prophecy which has become so popular today, is still not as old as the ECK-Vidya which was said to come out of the misty dawn of time in the northeast area of Tibet.

The term ECK-Vidya is generally employed to designate and indicate that great body of information, knowledge, prophecy and data for the individual ECK chela, concerning what is usually known as the Works of ECK and is that which must be used only for the past, present and future of the individual Soul, collective groups of Souls or a nation. It is the hidden, secret, arcane, esoteric, inner facts concerning the finer forces of the ECK powers, particularly the Soul or God powers of man. In former times we might apply the term magic to the ECK force, and the

35

knowledge included within it. The terms the living ECK Master and the Mahanta were held in highest regards by all concerned with ECKANKAR. As you see these terms were taken into hiding when the early religions, which included astrology in their agenda, started persecuting the followers of ECK because of its mighty force and wisdom.

All the tolerance which has been said about the Oriental religions and the mysteries of the Greeks adepts, as well as those of the West have disappeared under superstition, rites and ceremonies in order to survive. When ECK and ITS aspects including the ECK-Vidya became particularly too strong – as in Egypt during the period known as the Third Dynasty 2670-2600 B.C., under Djoser, one of the early Pharaohs who established the Step Pyramid – it was outlawed and had to go underground.

The priestcraft known as the Amon was responsible for this for they held the political power in Egypt during the ancient times. This was in the era of when Gopal Das, one of the early ECK Masters was then the head of ECKANKAR, here on earth. He later passed away and went into the heavenly worlds and was reassigned to the guardianship and teaching of the Shariyat-Ki-Sugmad, on the Astral plane. The Shariyat-Ki-Sugmad is the sacred book of ECKANKAR, and has been placed in the Temples of Golden Wisdom on each plane throughout the universes of God. Each Temple carries only a section of it so that the ECK chela when out of his body must be taken there by the living ECK Master who will in turn allow him to study under some past ECK Master who is respectively in charge of a section of the Shariyat-Ki-Sugmad.

However, by being underground during the many centuries, mainly forced there by the larger following of astrology, nothing could stop the ECK-Vidya from being passed on from Master to chela. The followers of ECK very carefully preserved the ancient wisdom, and today throughout the world it is still taught, but by a few, and to the few. In certain carefully guarded circles, among the ECK sages and seers, one must know how to give the right knock and he will be admitted to the ECK fellowship, and will be given the teachings to which he is entitled along certain lines. There are two proverbs which generally express truth, as follows, "When the chela is ready, the Master appears" and "When the Master approaches, the chela will know his footsteps."

This is more than true in ECKANKAR for many times when the

chela is ready the Mahanta, the living ECK Master, appears to him regardless of where he may be. Later, the chela meets the Master in the physical body. Naturally the casual chela, who is looking everywhere for truth, sees none of this. He sees only the far too common rank credulity and superstition among the great masses of people who have fallen from spiritual grace into the psychic trap, and look to astrology and clairvoyants to give them help.

The inner circle of ECK is not open to his inspection or entrance. He does not know how to give the right knock and the doors remain closed to him. Anyone who has penetrated the inner circle of ECKANKAR, and who has been admitted to the mysteries of the initiations, has come to know the difference between the ECK-Vidya and astrology.

Naturally it is an endless dispute among the spiritual authorities concerning the original source of the break between the ECK-Vidya and astrology. Some claim that it was in Egypt during the Third Dynasty when ECK had to go underground for its survival; others hold that the break came in India during the time of Manu, who made the first civil laws which later became many of the religious laws.

The principles of the ECK-Vidya are based upon the three followings things: (1) the ECK, or true spirit which is the ethereal substance pervading all the space and from which all material forms are produced and that upon which the Voice or the sounds of the SUGMAD are transferred throughout the universes of ITSELF. Within this media is stored every and all known lives of all Souls both in the material and spiritual worlds. (2) The secondary energies of ECK which animate and energize all the physical and solar universes. This is that part of the ECK called the Mind or Universal power which works mainly upon the Causal plane where all the records of the psychic bodies of man, individually, are stored and can be read by a few very good psychics, but not many are able to do this. (3) Last is the Akasha, the mind element in which all designs and plans are created in the Astral world and which penetrates the physical region where they are materialized in objective form through the action of visualization. It is here that the psychics and clairvoyants are mostly active in the reading of past lives between the astral and earth worlds, and predicting the future. This is an artificial type reading which means that hardly anyone touches the heart of the spiritual problems or karmic patterns of the individual Soul.

37

This is exactly what happens when the astrologer gives a reading to a client. He barely skims the surface and does not get into the real heart of the problem because he is working with the planetary vibrations. Unless one is exceedingly good at astrology and knows how to work out all the various positions on a chart through mathematics, he will more likely give his client a shallow reading. Nevertheless astrology reading will not cover any more than the guidelines of what might happen to a person. It can never be a positive reading because there is too much of the vibrations from the planets involved which might mean different wave lengths at different times which interfere with the chart the astrologer is trying to do on a client.

Often the ECKist will wear a charm and amulet for protection against certain forces and currents of the Kal force which could make him ill. He doesn't particularly believe in miracles, or supernatural happenings as the mass public does. The strange things which astonish the normal person the ECKist believes to be the work of natural energies which are put into action by unusual circumstances, or through the skill of someone who is an ECK adept at releasing this special energy to produce extraordinary phenomena. The ECKist also believes that a strong, steady thought concentrated upon an imagined thing can create the external reality and form of the idea.

The word HU which represents the mysterious and unknown name of God is chanted almost constantly by many an ECKist. There is not much literature devoted to the explanation of the word HU. It is said to be the ancient, secret name of God, which has been handed down through the ages by the ECK Masters, who are the members of the secret brotherhood, the Ancient Order of the Vairagi. Few persons outside the followers of ECKANKAR seem to know this name of God. Usually the ECKist refers to his God as the SUGMAD, but can chant either of the names for direct results from the divine Being.

The SUGMAD is said to be the ultimate of all Gods, even those which serve the orthodox religions. The ECKist also believes that life has four stages, birth, growth, decadence and extinction. Birth calls for no special joy nor does death denote any special sorrow. He also knows that a certain amount of time elapses between death and rebirth, that for forty-nine days the Soul of the departed is kept in a state of middle being. Only the ECK Masters and certain followers of ECK such as the Mahdis, the initiates of the Fifth plane, can break through this area of the forty-nine days and return or go into the higher worlds as desired.

One is reborn or passes into the next higher planes in either a happy or unhappy state according to the good or evil he has done in the previous existence of life. A person by his actions and thoughts creates a magnetic pull which leads him into his next existence of life. This is why those who are the ECKists, ones belonging to the ECKANKAR movement, have that happy opportunity of going beyond any of these lower planes into the higher worlds of existence which are the true spiritual worlds of the SUGMAD (God).

The living ECK Master always teaches that it is of vast importance for any chela at the edge of death not to think of material things; that it is most necessary at this time that one have pleasant happy thoughts. Those ECKists who attend the dying are concerned with the very last thoughts or words of the person, as this will give some indication as to what his rebirth will be. When death occurs, the ECK-Vidyist can be consulted as to where and on what the mind of the deceased rested in his last moments. The ECK-Vidyist decides what the contemplations of the individuals in the deceased's family and friends should be and which of the family should not be too close in the funeral arrangements because of the vibratory disharmonies.

This is an established fact and must be tied in with the individual's quest for identity. It is often that this quest cannot be fulfilled unless one first has the knowledge gained from the ECK-Vidya reading about himself. Of course love and compassion is the first stirring within of knowledge. No one is favored over the other. For every poison of the mind there is an antidote, for example, the antidote for ignorance is awareness and knowledge, which can come through the ECK-Vidya reading. For anger there can be loving kindness, but there is always the reverse or the antidote, and it's up to each to find it, and having found it, to use it.

The mystical symbolism relating to the Bhavachakra, which is the Wheel of Life, or that which those in ECK call the cycle of the ECK-Vidya, and the human organism holds an important position in this system of prophecy. In this connection, they form the body of the musical instrument, as it were, while the four elements, fire, water, air and earth constitute the strings. Man's body, where the ECK-Vidya is considered, is merely a sounding board for the notes struck by the heavenly musician during the performance of the opera. It will be noticed that fire, water, air and earth through the medium of their signs in the jewels of the months, especially the moonstone, jasper and sapphire, govern the central organs of the body. When these are in harmony with one another within their own spheres the whole bodily health is good.

While astrology acts only in the capacity of astral mediumship and casts gathered or reflected potencies into the magnetic atmosphere of man, they act only harmoniously or discordantly, according to the positions of the major planets. But the system of the ECK-Vidya only works in the beneficial area, for there is no place in the heavenly worlds for the negative qualities of man to express themselves.

Therefore man is like the five-pointed star. He has five points of projected energy which is constantly poured out by Soul, to the outer world. The hands, head and feet are the five points of projection from which the streams of vital force are constantly radiating. These are symbolized by the five-pointed star. There are also other positive centers within the body which give out the energies to the outer world. These are the brain, the spleen, the heart and the generative organs plus the solar plexus. Then too there are the eyes, the ears and the elimination organ for the body waste. This is actually twelve in all.

The brain, spleen, heart and solar plexus area is that which bears the brunt of most outgoing and incoming energies. When trouble or anxiety of mind crosses the individual's path he feels it in that part of the body called the pit of the stomach. This sensitive area is within the solar plexus and it is that which must be always kept in harmony with the rest of the body for it is the region of organs which keeps the gastric juices and sympathetic nervous system in good health.

The spiritual liberty of man depends somewhat upon the perfect freedom of the physical organism. Therefore, that which cramps, binds and warps the body out of its natural proportion is fatal to any real spiritual progress, because the inharmony of the actions of the spiritual forces of the body throws it out of kilter.

This is why the ECK-Vidya is important in the life of man, because it takes in consideration everything about him. It regards the spiritual structure of man and closely examines him as an organism as well as a Soul. The ECK-Vidya reader looks at the individual he is reading because he has been given permission to look into his aura and spiritual body. He sees that the client forms an oval or egg-shaped figure, which is beyond the physical, the narrow end being the feet, the broad end is the brain. This oval form makes up the magnetic atmosphere, and consists of twelve concentric rays of Soul force, each of which has a direct affinity with the other bodies of man and the creative principles of nature, and corresponds with the prismatic rays of the solar spectrum. Each zone or ray exercises a peculiar power of its own, and is pure according to its state of luminosity.

The ECK-Vidya reader can assert that any particular ray has the meaning that the person being read has either a benevolent character or that he is bad and has a sinful mannerism. Purity or impurity depends entirely on the bright color of the tint of any particular ray. From these colors are formed every conceivable shade and tint in the infinite variety of combinations found in the infinite variety of human beings; each and all depends on the ever-changing of Soul in the varied universes — also upon the corresponding magnetic states of the planes and universes at the respective moments of the individual's birth in this world.

The sound current with all its different notes and musical harmonies which can be heard on the various planes as separate sounds may come forth in the twelve rays of man. These are the vibrations which are attached to each individual Soul at the time of Its birth on this planet, and throughout each incarnation It has in the physical body as well as the psychic bodies which It retains and passes through in varied incarnations until It reaches the Atma (Fifth) plane where It is purified.

These are what one would observe who is doing the ECK-Vidya readings. These vibrations are visible to him in that they retain their special polarity for the whole existence of that particular Soul to whom they belong through Its existence in the lower worlds. These lower worlds are the psychic planes, physical, astral, causal, mental, and etheric. But once Soul has reached the Atma plane It becomes purified and the vibrations change. Thus the reader of the ECK-Vidya records must be aware that he is now reading a clear Soul and not the records of the lower lives. This is the division between the astrology reader and the ECK-Vidya reader, and few know and understand this at all. It is also the division between the psychic and clairvoyant readers and the ECK-Vidya. The former two can only read the physical records and misinterpret them for records in the unseen worlds.

The problem here is that so many do not understand the influence of illusion which is established by the Kal (negative) force in the five lower worlds, those which are under the Atma (Soul) realm. This world which is considered the psychic world ruled by the Universal Mind power, which is the psychic force and considered the God power by so many, is that which establishes the illusion.

Often illusion is called imagination. We do not speak of this word with contempt, for without it no pictures would be painted, no books written, no buildings planned and erected; in fact nothing would be created not even ourselves. If your parents had not fallen in love and succumbed to the illusion called love by some and sexual attraction by others, you would not be here.

Yet we know that living in this world is to have to deal with illusion. This is the basic feature which the ECK-Vidya reader has to understand when someone comes to him for a reading. He knows the ordinary young man who is in love with the ordinary young woman feels that it's the romance of the century. He knows that the young man who believes that he wants to help the human race by spreading the word of God, cannot do it alone and must have training to do so, and that the lunatic who claims that he is the incarnation of Christ or one of the chief disciples is a victim of this illusion of the Kal force.

He must sweep away all this illusion and speak the truth although there might be resentment which arises against him. He must be honest at all times with the client who sits before him and wishes only for a message of joy and happiness.

Of course not all illusion is love, and not all love is illusion, but the imaginary plays a great part in it. Most people fall in love not with a person but with their own ideas of that person. This is why most men or women never got over their first love, and always refer back to it as being in love with the ideal person. This is why so many people fall in love with their doctor, psychiatrist, or their Guru. This is the illusion established by the Kal, and as time strips off the glamour, the better and unrealized qualities of the person show through; or sometimes the worst qualities, and then there is the falling out of love.

This illusion has created problems for the human race, for many believe that power is greater than love. Because of this belief the whole human race has suffered since the beginning of its origin.

We find that there has never been a time when peace has been established universally upon this earth. The truth of the matter is that peace will never be established because of the Kal force. The Kal is a disturbing factor and its purpose here is to put each Soul through a series of tests to become purified until It passes through every psychic plane and finally reaches the Atma (Soul) plane where It becomes purified and able to have Self-Realization.

The background which is being laid down here is for the purpose of showing the individual just what takes place so that the ECK-Vidya reading is possible. Unless you have some of the background there is never a chance of understanding the ECK-Vidya reading and misunderstandings often arise.

The number twelve has profound significance in many areas of ECKANKAR, the Ancient Science of Soul Travel. It has been said that all of the human life, as well as the spiritual is attuned to this number. For example, every ECK Master who comes to this world generally has twelve disciples and the Mahanta, the living ECK Master, is always assured of picking twelve strong followers who will stay with him, out of seventy-two and who will give him assurance that the message of ECK will be carried on when he leaves the theater of worldly operations.

There are the twelve labors of every chela who struggles to achieve Mastership. There are the twelve jewels which represent the months of the year. There are twelve basic mineral salts in homeopathic medicines, and twelve not sixteen ounces to a pound of gold, also twelve inches to a foot of yardage. Diamond which is the basic jewel for the ECK-Vidya Wheel of Life, representing the month of Mokshove, August, has twelve sides or axes and must be cut along these lines. The Wheel of the ECK-Vidya consists of twelve spokes and twelve months make up the cycle in man's yearly life cycle. There is the twelve year cycle which makes up the full turn of the wheel in man's life so that he has a chemical change every cycle.

Therefore it's no surprise that in the ECK-Vidya there are twelve major experiences of Soul on the ECK-Vidya Bhavachakra Wheel of Life. Man must go through each of these before he becomes purified and able to journey to the true world of the SUGMAD in order to become a co-worker and receive his assignment in eternity for helping with all beings and mainly the human race.

If one begins life here in this universe in the month of Astik, which is that of the Emerald, or days of wisdom, known as January, he will experience that which is a different type than in the other months of the year of the ECK-Vidya. We can always look at this individual as being restless, and having problems with his own marriage or the marriage of his parents. This is the journey in which he learns courage for all his future incarnations. He will have one lac within this first sign of the Bhavachakra, the ECK-Vidya Wheel of Life. A lac is equivalent to one hundred thousand years. Eighty-four lacs amounts to eight million, four hundred thousand years.

The Awagawan, or the Wheel of Life, as it is sometimes called is the coming and going of Soul as It lives and operates under the Law of Karma. This wheel is a marvelous phenomena. The idea is that the individual accompanied by the mind and its load of karma moves through the endless ages, from birth to birth, passing through the eighty-four lacs of different kinds of living beings.

A wandering Soul, one who has not taken up ECKANKAR, often finds Itself passing from birth to birth, to make Its way through all of the tiresome and long lives which his karma calls for while in this world. There is no escape from this Wheel until one meets the Mahanta, the living ECK Master and learns to contact the ECK sound current.

The eighty-four lacs, or eight million, four hundred thousand lives, can be the fate of an individual Soul unless It meets with the Mahanta, the living ECK Master, regardless of what form that It may be in at the time. In regard to the eighty-four lacs it means that in this world there are many sorts of living beings, or species of living things. Of course this is only an approximate number of the exact types of living beings here.

They are somewhat as follows: Three million species of plant life; Two million, seven hundred thousand kinds of insect species; One million, four hundred thousand kinds of birds; Nine hundred thousand kinds of water animals; and four hundred thousand kinds of land animals, men and others just above men, such as angels, demons and others.

This makes eight million, four hundred thousand, each with its uncounted millions of individuals. A Soul may pass through all of these or only part of them, but in all cases it depends upon Its karma. In some cases It may begin life as man and stay as man until the finish of it, through a large number of incarnations, up until the finish of Its time here on earth. This latter depends upon the fact of whether It has met the Mahanta, the living ECK Master, in a past life and left him, then accepts him again in this present life, as the only Master who can lift It into the heavenly worlds.

The rounds of all these lives constitutes the Wheel of Life. It depends upon the individual entirely as to how many of these lives he may have to pass through. But as stated before no one ever escapes from this Wheel of Life until he has met the Mahanta, the living ECK Master, and learns to contact the ECK sound current.

There are four kinds of karma which are attached to the individual and must be worked off before man can leave this life permanently. Every ECK-Vidya reader can see this karma and knows what is in store for the individual who is being read. First, is that called the Adi Karma, which is the primal karma. When Soul enters into this world for the first time and is born into a body It has no karma. But It begins Its life in the regions of mind and matter. Therefore the primal karma consists of the action of the creative force, the ECK sound current, whose function, among others duties, is to bring Souls into the material planes in order that They may begin to accumulate experience.

In other words It begins to acquire experience on Its own initiative. This means It begins to establish an individual law of Its own life, Its own world and to create Its own destiny. It begins to enjoy, suffer, to reap rewards and to pay penalties. This is the beginning of Its own karma, and It has inaugurated Its long series of earthly lives. By each and every act, from that time on It stores up karma. Even when It is least active, It is still making karma, and in all this activity, Its mind body is the chief instrument for creating karma through the law of cause and effect.

The second type of karma is called the Praabdh, which means the fate karma. It is that which has been earned in one or more previous lives, and upon which this present life is based. Because this type of karma must be met and paid for by the individual, it is seldom that the Mahanta, the living ECK Master, will ever destroy it.

The third type of karma is called Sinchit Karma. This means the reserve karma. It could be compared to money which has been put in the bank as a savings account. It is drawn upon only at the will of the Lord of Karma, and not by the will of the individual. The

Lord of Karma may draw on this reserve karma for the individual and determine it to be lived out at such times and places as he may determine, and the individual has nothing to say about it, nor can he prevent it.

The fourth kind of karma is the Kriyaman Karma, the daily new karma. It is that sort of karma which the individual makes from hour to hour and day to day during his lifetime. This sort of karma may be disposed of in any of the following ways. Man might suffer, or reap its rewards at once good or bad, or at some other time in his life. He may also have it stored up as Sinchit Karma to be drawn upon at some future time, according to the will of the Lord of Karma. In this case, it can become fate karma for the individual's next life.

It can be said here that when the Mahanta, the living ECK Master, takes over the life of any follower, that is the chela or follower surrenders totally to the Mahanta, the karma of that disciple alters considerably. His whole destiny undergoes a complete change. This however all depends entirely upon the will of the living ECK Master, for then the Master is the individual's karmic lord. As the Mahanta is superior to all other lords of the various worlds, he may do whatsoever he pleases with the karma of his disciple.

As a rule he does not interfere with the karma of his disciple, until the latter has reached the Fifth (Soul) plane and has become a Mahdis through the initiations of ECKANKAR. In this case he will help the disciple to release all four types of karma at once, through working them off in this lifetime. If the individual finds himself obliged to endure more than he can hardly stand, he must remember that the living ECK Master is doing all that is possible to clean up the follower's karma and as quickly as possible. When his life ends here on earth, he will be free forever.

When the living ECK Master does this it is out of great love, knowing that the disciple will at last be free. When this happens he should be thankful that the living ECK Master has put him through all at once and finished it. However, the ECK Master will never allow the burdens to become too heavy and often he even bears some of the karmic burdens himself out of his great love and sympathy for the individual. In any case, the living ECK Master always does what he knows is best for the chela, for he is himself the embodiment of living kindness for all who follow him and all life itself.

The first journey of Soul is one in which appearance is important and esoteric truths are downgraded. There is belief in one's self plus the rugged determination to achieve victory.

The second journey will come during the era of the bloodstone, called Uturat, or days of love. The symbol here is a bag of gold surrounded by the bloodstone jewels. There is a great concern for love, companionship and wealth. Soul doesn't want to travel alone but links all objectives and aims with another. There is a sharing of joys, victories and problems. There is a great giving of love but a greater need for love to be returned. Also there is a capacity to rationalize one's own faults to a great extent.

The third step on the path is that which comes during the time of the jade, in the era of Garvata, or days of joy. This is the time when Soul is restless, and has a great sense of urgency. Although there is some dissatisfaction It has great joy in finding another Soul which fills the gaps of unity, and brings high degrees of happiness.

On the other hand if this Soul doesn't find his spiritual twin during this era he can become strongly influenced by the mind (Kal) power and disappointed in the whole of life. He can be out of step with all society, highly critical, and express his disappointments strongly. But on the whole he is a happier person than this because of his sense of humor.

The fourth step on the path is that of the opal, called Ebkia, or the days of hope. This is the period in which the primary search is for peace, as though Soul is tired by the experiences of the first three steps on the path. There is a need to give up the outer struggle and find all the answers first within oneself.

There is a great sensitivity to one's own environment, and anything that needs adjusting to something new and different such as travel or moving into a new home. There is a strong feeling for traditions, conventional things and a belief that it's possible to work out one's own destiny without material challenges or physical activity. There is a magnificent sense of hope that everything is going to turn out all right without questioning one's self or others.

The fifth step of the path is that of the sapphire, called Ralot, or the days of truth. This is the time when Soul bargains and barters and there is a need for the outward manifestation of Its inner search. These are the days of truth when Soul never doubts that It belongs on the throne. Napoleon never doubted that he was destined to be the emperor of France, and that he was the incarnation of Alexander the Great. General George Patton, Jr. believed that he was the incarnation of Napoleon and destined to be the military leader of all World War II. Other famous examples could be given if there was room to spare in this book.

But it is here that Soul develops the strong belief in Itself along with that of self-importance. It is a heady period in which there is materialistic achievements, joy, recognition and personal power.

The sixth step on the path is that of the moonstone, called Sahak, or the days of music. This is the period in which Soul has passed through the journey of power and recognition and seeks a pleasant resting place where he can work out his destiny in peace and quiet. There is no idleness but one of strong feeling for birth and rebirth, for generation of inner and personal power.

Peace and harmony come to him, great demonstrations of kindness and harmony with gratitude of what has been given Soul comes in this era. It is like music to Soul.

The seventh step on the path is that of the ruby, called Kamitoc, or the days of freedom. This is when freedom comes through knowledge as given on the other planes by the guardians of the Shariyat-Ki-Sugmad, the holy books of ECKANKAR. There are indications that Soul is conscious of what can and what cannot be done, and has definite plans and purposes. Those on this step can experience deep esoteric realization and make genuine contributions to the spiritual movement of the times.

The eighth step on the path is that which is of great awareness of Soul. It is the era of the diamond, call Mokshove, or days of light. It represents the challenge of secrets, translation of spiritual knowledge into great truths. But Soul absorbs whatever knowledge and lessons are to be learned here and often undergoes remarkable changes. However, the answers which Soul seeks often plague It, and It investigates, challenges the spiritual needs for survival in the world of God. It is a step which is difficult to get through but generally that Soul which has gone this far will do so.

The ninth step on the path is that which is known as the period of the agate, called Dzyani, or the days of friendship. This is the testing journey in which Soul can achieve all the lower worlds, and much the upper has to offer. It is a journey of high success, power, rewards, achievements and splendor. This is the time when Soul can meet with material defeat yet go on to be successful in very many spiritual things in the sense that it brings knowledge that there is always another step to take, that the quest for God-Realization seems to have no end.

The tenth step on the path is that of the jasper, called Parinama, or the days of beauty. This is the quiet period in which Soul finds that striving for the common good and not for glory and honor is the ultimate goal. There is a feeling of isolation, caused by imperfections in Soul Itself when It has not reached purification. This is the time for Soul to understand the sublime, yet simple understanding that the journey in eternity is endless, changing, that nothing is quite enough on what appears to be a never-ending quest for liberation. Yet through all this Soul is constantly faced with the beauty of life and this keeps It moving toward God.

The eleventh step on the path is that of the pearl, called Hortar, or the days of wealth. Soul now begins to see and feel liberation from the other steps on the path of ECKANKAR. It has the tendency to fly away and to leave behind all binding ties. Soul now wants to rid Itself of this body if possible, and the search becomes more intense via the Mahanta, the living ECK Master.

There is a willingness to surrender the things of the past and follow the living ECK Master. Most of those at this step are imbued with high ideals and a wide sense of freedom; they are emotional, sensitive, easily hurt and easily put off.

The twelfth step on the path is that of onyx, called Niyamg, or the days of charity. It is that period in which the mystery of life resolves itself and Soul has found Itself in the larger scheme of things. Soul has reached the completion of the Wheel of Life. There is no more for It to seek for now the value of life is laid out of it. The glamour and grandeur of the world means nothing to It, and It desires now to enter into the true heavenly state to become a co-worker with God.

CHAPTER 4

THE ZIQUIN OF THE ECK-VIDYA

As explained in Chapter Two the Ziquin of the ECK-Vidya means above the psychic planes. Zi is the Amdo language word for above, and quin means five. Thus it has the meaning of being above the five planes. This is the Atma or the Fifth plane from which all ECK-Vidya readings are made.

It is for this very reason that few persons in this world can do a pure ECK-Vidya reading. Generally it's the Mahanta, the living ECK Master, who is now serving in this world as the spiritual director of ECKANKAR, who does this type of reading. However, he always lifts several chelas into the Atma plane (Fifth) and there through a series of initiations they eventually become the Mahdis, or initiates of the Fifth world. Some of these are able to give the ECK-Vidya readings. Not all are capable because their talents do not run in this direction. However, there should be one or two who are able to do the ECK-Vidya readings, but it's always through the power of the Mahanta granted to the Mahdis to do the ECK-Vidya.

The Ziquin is not always the Wheel of Life, although some often consider it to be. It is really the smaller wheel or that which represents the five psychic planes of the lower worlds. These are the physical, astral, causal, mind and etheric (subconscious). When one starts out to resolve all his karmic problems he must take into consideration that his karma must be resolved on each of these planes before he can enter into the heavenly worlds, which begin at the Atma or Soul plane, which is often called the Fifth. This is really the dividing line between the psychic worlds and the spiritual regions. The mental plane is usually considered a singular whole plane which includes the etheric plane so that we call them the psychic planes with only four in number.

The ECK-Vidya is the only reading which can give the lives of the individual Soul on each plane. Many people hardly ever get above the astral, yet it is possible that some will be able to get into the higher planes while still living in this worldly life on earth. My point here is that only those who have been initiated in ECK can receive the fifth initiation which gives them the opportunity of entering into the Soul plane. Each initiation is tied into the plane which it respectively represents.

In other words the initiations go like this: The first plane is called the Acolyte, or the dream state or material world initiation. The second is the Arahata, or the astral plane initiation. The third is the Ahrat, or the causal plane initiation. The fourth, is the Chiad, the mental plane initiation, the fifth is the Mahdis, the fifth plane initiation, which is the first in the true spiritual worlds.

There are eight other initiations which start in the heavenly worlds and go above those named: The Shraddha is the initiate of the sixth plane which is Alakh Lok; the Bhakti is the initiate of the seventh plane which is the Alaya Lok; the Gyanee is the initiate of the eighth plane which is known as the Hukikat Lok; the Maulani is the initiate of the ninth plane which is the Agam Lok; the Adepiseka is the initiate of the tenth plane which is the Anami Lok; the Kevalshar is the eleventh plane which is the Ocean of Love and Mercy or the SUGMAD world; the Maharaji is the twelfth initiate which is the true world of the home of the SUGMAD, the living Reality, and the Mahanta Maharai, is the initiate of the God or SUGMAD Realization, which covers all worlds.

Very few including the ECK chelas have gone any further than the seventh plane in this life. Those who have developed spiritually enough generally reach the eighth or maybe the ninth and must work spiritually throughout the whole universes. Even though one might reach the God-Realization plane and become the Mahanta, he will keep unfolding. Spiritually he is free of all karma but long as he is living in a human body there will be physical troubles because he is taking on the karma of many of his own chelas, and often the complete universe of the psychic worlds.

Therefore the Ziquin is most important in the lives of every chela on the path of ECKANKAR because it is concerned with the basic karma of the individual and the ECK-Vidya reader is spiritually developed enough to be able to divide the true from the false and give a reading which will be very accurate. So many find that a reader such as a clairvoyant or psychic is not accurate in the sense that each is reading only the physical records, or working with symbols.

The only symbols which the lower worlds have is that of the precious stones. For example there are several which represent each plane respectively: The emerald represents the physical world; the bloodstone represents the astral world; the jade represents the causal world, and the opal represents the mental world.

These are parts which make up the doctrine of the Ziquin for each represents a part of man's nature respectively, and are accounted for in the Books of the Shariyat-Ki-Sugmad. This means these are the stones of the mystical sides of the worlds which belong to the psychic part of man. His various bodies, such as the physical, astral, causal, mental and etheric are those which make up his entire being. The emerald is the sign of the physical being of man; it includes beauty but green in color is the material part which is the color of nature. The bloodstone is the color of the astral plane and represents the element of emotional love and the darker sides of nature. The jade represents the causal plane and is the color of the time track which gives the past lives which determine the present life of the individual. Last the opal represents the mental world with its milky coloring. The black opal represents the subconscious mind which is the secondary part of the mental world.

These are the planes of the psychic worlds which everybody must be contented to deal with until Soul reaches that state of spiritual unfoldment in the Atma (Fifth) plane. It also represents the first four months of the year for the ECK-Vidya, which is given in Chapter Two. These months are: The month of the emerald, known as Astik, or the days of wisdom; the month of the bloodstone, called Uturat, or days of love; the month of the jade, called Garvata, or days of joy, and the month of the opal called Ebkia, or days of hope.

We are then concerned with symbols within the year of the twelve year cycle. These are again, the Year of the Fierce Winds; the Year of the Bright Snows; the Year of the Brilliant Sun; the Year of the Beautiful Flowers; the Year of the Full Moon; the Year of the Strange Storms; the Year of the Wandering Seas; the Year of the Bountiful Earth; the Year of the Abundant Fruits; the

Year of the Raging Fires; the Year of the Lavish Grains, and the Year of the Trembling Leaf.

As stated previously each year we change in nature, and have to meet a new set of conditions. Thus the full cycle runs sometimes in the order of 144 to 150 years, as often an individual cycle might go more than twelve years. Actually this should be the life expectancy of every individual on earth but the development of science and other factors in man's life have shortened it considerably.

During the ancient days only the giants dwelled here upon earth, before the creation of man. This world was a paradise for every living creature could maintain and preserve its survival through the fruitfulness of the earth. The world was furnished with inhabitants; the first age was that of innocence and happiness, called the Satya Yuga, the Golden Age. In this age truth and right prevailed, though not enforced by law, nor were there any magistrate or courts to threaten or punish. The forest had not been robbed of its trees to furnish timbers for ships, nor had men build fortifications round their towns. There were no such things as swords, spears, or helmets. The earth brought forth all things necessary for man, without his labor in ploughing or sowing. Perpetual spring reigned, flowers sprang up without seed, the rivers flowed with milk and wine, and yellow honey distilled from the oaks.

Then succeeded the Tretya Yuga, the Silver Age. Inferior to the Golden Age we find that the spring was shortened, and the year divided into seasons. Then, for the first time man had to endure the extremes of heat and cold, and houses became necessary. Caves were the first dwellings, and leafy coverts of the woods and huts woven from twigs and leaves. Crops would no longer grow without planting, and the farmers were obliged to sow the seed, and using the ox and horse to draw the plough as they toiled the fields.

Next came the Dwapara Yuga or what we know as the Copper or Brass Age. Men became more savage of temper and ready to take up arms at the drop of a stone. They saw their neighbors succeeding where they could not and often attacked to have grain or the wealth their neighbors had collected.

The Kali Age or that known as the Iron Age is the one in which we are living today. It is the worst and hardest of all ages. Crime has burst like a flood over the world; modesty, truth and honor have dissolved and in their places have come fraud and cunning, violence and the wicked love of gain.

The first three ages have already elapsed and we are now living in the last which began at midnight between the 17th and 18th of February 3102 B.C. The duration of each age is said to be, respectively, the Satya Yuga, 1,728,000; the Tretya Yuga, 1,296,000; the Dwapara Yuga, 864,000, and the Kali Yuga, 432,000 years of man. The descending numbers represent a similar physical and moral deterioration of men in each age; the four yugas comprise an aggregate of 4,320,000 of our years, and constitute a great yuga or mahayuga.

This is the Mahayuga, or the Manvantaras, which is the Sanskrit for cycle in cosmic history. The current manvantara embraces the Kali Yuga in which we are living now. This is one tenth of the duration of the cycle, of the present era. Man tries to establish law and order but this is the time that the Kal has its greatest influence. Soul must struggle through each of the eras and at the end of this cosmic cycle It will, if It hasn't reached perfection and entered into the heavenly worlds, be put into a deep sleep or coma, lifted up into the heavenly worlds, and kept in this state for a duration of many years. Meanwhile the lower or psychic states will be destroyed and all the lower worlds now gone, the space left will be in silence and darkness until the SUGMAD decides to re-establish them again. Then those Souls which had been put into sleep will start their journey over again to reach perfection.

Thus one begins to think in three cycles when he looks at the ECK-Vidya records: First there is the daily cycle which begins at midnight with the minutes and hours that make up the karmic pattern of releasing karma or gathering it for the individual Soul. There is so much karma being given off daily and so much gathered. The whole trick of the matter is to balance out this karma, so that it doesn't show either too much bad nor too much good.

The second cycle is that of the yearly which is concerned with the monthly pattern of one's individual life. This is also part of the gathering and throwing off of karma to balance and assist Soul to perfection. The files of Soul's journeys through many lives show up here when one looks at the monthly records, but not as much as the twelve month periods. We find these useful in the readings of one's ECK-Vidya records because it's a part of that which makes up the whole. These records start with Astik, the month of

55

the emerald, and ends with Niyamg, the month of the onyx.

Both of these cycles are very important. The minute and hourly will give one's deeper action within the law of cause and effect. The yearly is important because it works toward the long range reading of what the future might be because of the past.

The third is the twelve year cycle which makes up the life of the individual Soul. Where and what is the full extent of the individual Soul within a body? It means therefore that Soul will have only a certain period of time in each body that it takes on during any and each incarnation. Man's personal longevity comes to just about six or less cycles within one body, so it means that he is not capable under the reign of the Kali Yuga to live out his full life span. Of course this is the physical and moral degeneration of the individual since the era of the Golden Age, when man lived in what was then the perfect body. But he has learned that he cannot go back to that state until he has turned back and sought perfection again, through Soul unfoldment.

The full Soul records are in the cycles which consist of the cosmic periods of man. He must go through a certain amount of these periods between birth and death. This is where most of his karma is gathered and resolved, but after coming under the Mahanta, the living ECK Master, most of his karma is balanced so that he can enter into the heavenly worlds at the end of his life and never have to return again.

The ECK-Vidya reader must use the Saguna Sati which is the method of instant projection used by the ECK Masters, for reading of these Soul records. The files are fanned out like that of playing cards before him; there are millions of them, and he must use his own spiritual discrimination in order to pick out the best for the readee.

He realizes that there are three ways that the Soul records may be read; these are generally called as follows: First, the golden road, which is the middle path, or those which will give the readee only the highest spiritual type of reading. This is concerned with Soul's progress only through a certain series of incarnations, and never with anything else. The second is the silver road, which is the right hand path in which the reader gives only the lives of the individual Soul on each plane through a certain series of incarnations and Its unfoldment through its inner bodies, astral, causal and mental.

The third is the bronze road, which is the left hand road which is negative road or that of the material body. It is the readings which include only that of the physical lives which Soul has to go through, and its future in the earth world. The unfoldments which are concerned with the physical bodies are not very developed, therefore the readee is getting only a partial understanding of his past lives and future.

It is best for the individual to get a full reading which would include a part of each road, or the different lives that Soul goes through on the various planes of the universe before reaching the state of perfection. It gives more understanding of what his life is all about, and certainly does give him a grasp on what his mission as a co-worker with God may be in time.

This means then that the reader who uses the ECK-Vidya method must go into a state of light trance, or perhaps none if he desires to reach that state whereby the records are available for him to read. As said before he will use the Saguna Sati, that method of instant projection used by the ECK Masters for reading the Soul records.

He can do this with his eyes open, and fully in consciousness within this physical world. He can do this while walking about the room, or by sitting in a chair. The first thing that he must do regardless is to still the mind, by looking at the screen of the inner mind which should be absolutely blank.

We assume that the reader takes an easy chair first, and takes a few minutes either talking with the readee very quietly, or that he closes his eyes for a few moments, takes some deep breaths and then looks at the blankness of the mental screen within his mind.

By this time he is ready for the movement of Soul into the Atma (Fifth) plane where It will begin the research of seeking out the proper data for the readee.

He sets himself mentally for the projection from the back of the head. He counts up to three and moves quickly to three to ten feet behind the head, then he establishes where to go to read the records of the individual who has requested the reading.

Often times these records might be stored in different places on the Atma plane, because of the difference in individuality of the readee. There are at least five varied places where the records are filed. All lower plane records are stored within the varied bodies of the individual such as the physical, astral, causal and mental, and often the etheric plane. The other records which are the overall records and that of the higher regions are placed within the Atma, the Fifth plane, but here sometimes they are put in varied places for the benefit of the individual.

If he has become a Mahdis, an ECK initiate of the Fifth plane, then he would find his records on the Fifth plane in a region known as the Mearp, which is a part of the heavenly state where those who have reached this world by initiation often dwell. If he has been initiated into the Sixth plane, known as the Shraddha initiation, these records are kept in a section of the Atma region known as the Anuga.

The records of those initiates, the Bhakti, the Seventh plane initiation, the Gyanee, the Eighth plane initiation, the Maulani, the Ninth plane initiation, the Adepiseka, the Tenth plane, the Kevalshar, the Eleventh plane, and the Maharaji, the Twelfth plane are all kept in an area known as the ECK Nida region.

The Mahanta Maharai, or the ECK Master, which is the complete initiation or the circle of perfection has his records kept in the Sat Nam of Itself, which is the abode of the ruler of the Fifth plane, and the first manifestation of God. Because of his gigantic and awesome appearance, which is in the form of man, those who have come to this plane believe this is the SUGMAD (God) Itself. This is not true for he is only a manifestation of God.

All rulers of the various planes from the Atma down to the physical, in the spiritual hierarchy, have the appearance of the male, and not the female. This is why God is considered to be masculine according to the writers of the sacred literature. Few if any persons outside of ECKANKAR have been able to travel spiritually beyond the planes of the lower world. That is beyond the Atma or Fifth, one does not encounter any rulers in the seen state, but these are in spirit only and cannot be approached except through spirit.

The reader travels immediately to the region in which the Soul records of this individual have been stored, and can read more accurately and understandingly for him. It is a matter of knowing where these records are stored from the beginning of the reading, by communication with the Atma world before getting out of the body. The communication is simple for anyone who has learned the art of the ECK-Vidya readings. But for those who have not the reading might turn out to be a confusion of three or four other Souls mixed up and gives the readee a mixup which could even be harmful.

This has nothing to do with the aura, nor healing, for these are

58

different subjects altogether. The living ECK Master seldom reads auras unless he finds it necessary and more often if invited to do so. He certainly doesn't go in for aura balancing as this is somewhat a figment of the imagination. Auras do not change with any outside influence but only when there is change of the inner self, or spiritual difference within the individual. It is seldom that any psychic influence can reach the heart of the problem. Those who are recipients of aura balancing and who state that it made them feel better or some sort of thing like this are only under the illusion of the Kal forces.

Once the records of the individual Soul have been found in the proper place within the Atma (Fifth) plane, the reader of them must pull out what he believes is correct for the readee. He fans them out like a huge deck of cards on a table, and starts looking them over with the spiritual eyes for he is traveling in Atma Sarup, which is the Soul body, and works through the varied bodies such as the etheric, mental, causal, and physical to reach the proper sources which can communicate with the readee.

In other words his communication lines are through the silver cord which is attached to each of the varied bodies which he carries with him regularly, except for the Atma Sarup (Soul body). When he sheds his spirito-materialistic bodies in the mental worlds, the silver cord is also left behind, and he travels only in the Atma Sarup (Soul body). However, he must maintain contact with the last body such as the mental, in order to send the message through which goes along the lines of communication of the lower bodies to eventually reach the physical form, and uses the vocal cords or hand to write out the message which is being read by Soul on the Atma Lok (the Soul plane).

A good reading should take about an hour or two, but there is often quite a bit of research to do and the reader must be very careful. This is why a good ECK-Vidya reader wants to give a reading by written report or by tape. He knows that if he should be sitting in the presence of an individual and giving a report that questions might throw him off by disturbing his concentration. When he is in the state of reading it's best not to question nor be restless because this could create a disturbance in the inner worlds and mistakes could be made.

No reading is given except in the light. It is not like a general reading by a spiritualist medium which is so often done in complete darkness. However, the light of the room and the windows being raised with the shades up has nothing to do with the reading. Noises flowing in from the outside are usually disregarded unless they are loud and unusual.

The reader must be truthful therefore he must have time to work out the answers to what he knows the readee has requested. Therefore he knows that it will take time and if the readee has the patience then he will have truth given him. Sometimes it hurts to give truth to the readee, whom it's known is very sensitive. But it's better to do it this way rather than to say things which will build the ego of the individual.

This is one of the great problems of those giving readings: they know that for most of the people who come to them especially for past life readings it's more of a social thing than wanting truth. Since the readee has no social status in life he wants to be able to stand up with others who are socially prominent by claiming that he was a great historical figure in the past, perhaps Lincoln, Napoleon or Washington. This is sometimes akin to the family ancestry which many persons have specialists in making up family trees do for them. This is what is known in psychology as the ego-builder. When a reader tells anyone that she was Cleopatra in a past life it's generally an ego-builder, or patronizing the readee. This is in the field of materialism and no one who does readings should attempt anything of this nature for it's only another violation of the spiritual law and the reader will suffer if giving a white lie, even though it's to make the person feel better.

There are too many people who believe that they are the reincarnation of Jesus or some of the disciples, perhaps Abraham Lincoln and other historical characters, who are doing an injustice in this world. Once while visiting in Sarasota, Florida, I was asked by a person who had very good intentions and wasn't at all naive about life, if I would like to visit with Mary, the mother of Jesus. My curiosity got the best of me, and I was given the explanation that Mary was living on the edge of the city in a not too prosperous suburb. The lady who was giving the invitation became quite upset when I refused.

The point which I am trying to make here is that those great spiritual figures who lived in the past including many of the historical persons, are on the higher planes working with Souls to give them a greater spiritual unfoldment. They have not returned to this world because they are busy in their own sphere of spiritual influence.

It is a mistake to try to call upon them for spiritual assistance for this means they must turn away from their duties on the higher plane to this world and help those who have called on them. This takes times away from their duties on the higher planes, and often it might interfere with their work. Also it could not be of the best interest for either the petitioner or the petitioned because it may be possible that the saint whom one calls upon may have to stay in this realm for a considerable time before his manifested body for this particular plane can be resolved. In other words this story given here will clarify what I am saying.

In an authentic ashram for yoga training in India, several years ago, a group of young yogis got together and decided to call upon one of their saints to appear. The experiment was successful, but the saint scolded them for taking him away from his duties on one of the invisible planes. He stated that it would take considerable time, according to earth years, to resolve the manifested body and return to his original spirit body in which he was doing his work on the other plane of existence.

Therefore we must be careful of what one does when reading the ECK-Vidya records. The inexperienced may run into problems which he doesn't understand. In these days and times it's considered, by the teachings of the metaphysicians, that we can have anything in life provided we make the right contact with God. This is exactly the excuse that the metaphysical teacher gives, when the student approaches him and says that he has had no success in life. He is told that he has not made the right contact with God. Poor excuse indeed because the way to God is long and arduous and contact with IT is something that makes one forget all the material requests and comforts of life.

Whenever one believes that he has made contact with God, it is usually the Kal Niranjan, the negative God, of the lower worlds, who can at times fulfill the request as long as it's a material one. This is the way of deception for the requestee will have to pay for his gain some way or other. This is the law of Karma, the law of cause and effect.

The ECK-Vidya differs from astrology because it works in straight lines with the simple techniques of ECKANKAR, the Ancient Science of Soul Travel. Astrology involves angles, and must divide everything into parts and uses planetary magnetic fields and the angles of planets and constellations.

The ability to reach the state of reading the ECK-Vidya records of any individual is not easy, for it takes sometimes years, and perhaps many lifetimes of one to reach the state of being able to do this. Life itself is largely a struggle in which people employ the known such as astrology and other prediction methods to conquer the unknown. Most people are engaged in some sort of method to predict the future for the purpose of meeting with it more successfully. One must remember that he is not dealing with social trends nor historical environments nor, of course, the planetary systems to read the ECK-Vidya records in order to learn how life itself influences the individual. It certainly shows any ECK-Vidya reader that karma has shaped the present of the individual rather than any of the materialistic influences which the mantic sciences try to prove constantly.

When an individual changes his own future it is due to him making up his mind that it can be done. Too many people lean too heavily upon hypnosis, astrology and other mantic sciences to give them an assured future along certain paths. One is never in control of his own destiny if he does this. He, upon his own accord, should be able to determine his future and work toward it. Whenever the mantic sciences become too great in a world, it means that the world is on its downward fall and will soon end at the last of the yugas, if it is not already in it. This will bring about the destruction of the lower worlds and all that is in it unless the living beings and creatures are put into a comatic sleep and lifted into the Atma lok (Fifth plane) to stay in their coma until these worlds are rebuilt again for all life.

Whenever anyone has a reading by the ECK-Vidya he must be able to grasp the insight which is given him via the reader. There are often statements which appear to be misleading to the reader when there is a time element involved, or when one thinks in terms of what was said. For example, a woman once wrote about her son who disappeared on a large body of water while fishing. She believed that he was alive and well, but the ECK-Vidya records showed that this wasn't true. Her faith was in the fact that someone told her that he had been seen somewhere else, and that he had an argument with the authorities on the lake over fishing rights and was afraid of returning home. The truth was this chap fell overboard and drowned, and the answer given me was that "she would see him soon, talk with him, and learn the truth."

Months later she wrote an indignant letter that I had been wrong and that in a dream she had talked with her son and he gave her the true story about his death. She made the claims that I was not truthful in telling her about her son's accident. But this is the way that I was instructed to tell through the ECK-Vidya and nothing else could be done.

This is typical of all those who give readings and work in the field of prophecy. Divination plays a strange role when it surfaces through the vocal messages. The answers to questions are often so ambiguous that few people can understand them, but the oracle or the reader usually proves to be correct.

The classic example of this ambiguity was the case of Croesus, King of Lydia, 560-540 B.C., who inquired of the oracle whether or not he would be victorious in a war he proposed to wage against the Persians. The answer given was, "Croesus, having crossed the river Halys, will destroy a great kingdom." Croesus interpreted this to mean that he would destroy the kingdom of his enemy; but, instead, he destroyed his own kingdom, for he was defeated by the Persians under Cyprus the Great and taken prisoner. When he was subsequently released, he complained to the priests of Delphi, for having given him a prediction which had failed. But the priests, however, maintained that the oracle had correctly predicted the results of his actions, that was the downfall of a great kingdom, and that Croesus was at fault because he had misinterpreted the oracle.

This misinterpretation is often put wrong by the individual who makes a request of anyone who is capable of divination. Once a woman came to me in complaint about the wrong interpretation of a mystic reader who had said that her husband who was in bad health would be well and happy within six months. Instead he died in this period of time. I instantly researched the ECK-Vidya records and found that the mystic was right. The husband was now well and happy and living on the astral plane. I told this to the woman but she was still unhappy and would not accept the answer which meant that she could not make up her mind of what was truth.

Anyone who gets an ECK-Vidya reading may get certain answers which seem ambiguous and the reader is forced to give them to the individual who has requested the reading. It is advisable that the readee consider the reading very carefully and not be looking constantly for something which means his future is filled with happiness and prosperity. In other words, look for what is hidden in the veiled statement. Every statement should be weighed in the ECK-Vidya reading, well as other readings. This is why the reading should always be a written one so that the readee will have an opportunity to go over it carefully and study each sentence with diligent understanding.

This is true for both past incarnations and future ones. Those who receive a reading which seems to have meanings for past incarnations with certain ambiguities must establish the same problem: what do these statements really mean? One doesn't take a strange dream literally, but either goes to the right source – a book or someone who can, in his opinion, interpret the dream right. Therefore he must think in the same terms as the future and how are the statements made about his own past incarnations going to effect whatever lives or present future he must be engaged in at the time any comes about.

All this comes up with certain elements which the reader must consider, and the readee certainly must understand. These are his present character traits. What are they and how are they going to effect the individual at this moment? This is important for it is the consideration of what we call the prediction and control of phenomena. Anyone who is weak in will power certainly doesn't expect to be able to have much discipline in making changes within himself. However, the training in discipline which he can receive while serving as a chela under the living ECK Master, will certainly help in building his will power.

Therefore we must consider the various types who are engaged in the trade of prediction and prophecy. These are clairvoyants, mediums, mystics, psychics, spiritualists, astrologers and ECK-Vidya readers. What is to be considered here is the character traits of these individuals who do varied types of reading. One must consider just what aberrations does a reader have if any and will he be looking at any of these aberrations when giving a reading. Is he basically honest and telling the truth when having to decide what is best to tell the readee? These are all important for the readee in order to get the best for what he is seeking.

Next, it's best for the readee not to say too much nor for him to ask too many questions for many a reader is what is known as a cold reader. This is a shrewd, well knowledgeable person who finds his client overanxious and willing to talk. In fact he often persuades his client to talk, in hopes of finding something to hang a peg upon in order to start giving him a means by which to hang his predictions.

After a few minutes of talk, and a good guess about the client from his clothes, face and other things he can begin to put together the problems which the individual faces. Then he starts talking and generally gets ninety percent right in most cases. There is nothing wrong with this kind of reader except that he is only a poor surface reader, and cannot get any further than next week's or next month's predictions.

The next thing to point out is that often the reader might make a time element on the client's predictions. Sometimes these are time predictions such as an accident in three weeks, or something of this nature pinpointed to the exact time of day or date that it will happen. It has been pointed out that some of the most famous psychics have pinpointed certain dates for major disasters somewhere in the world. For example, Edgar Cayce whose prediction that the west coast of the United States was going to have a gigantic earthquake and certain sections disappear under water, seemed to have been pinpointed for a special date and it never happened.

It has left many people confused and unhappy, and certainly disappointed in their own particular case when expecting the good to come about and it never did according to the prediction made. But one should always remember that pinpointing a prediction or a major happening in time is the hardest of all parts in the field of divination. Many times the person giving the prediction cannot see very well what the time element is and must guess at it, or give what he sees. This is wrong, but often the pressure by the client forces him to give a time element to certain predictions, and he may give what is known in his area but it's not for the best as it's only a hazardous guess.

Also the time element may shift according to events which might get in the way, or the changing of the mind of the client, who is all important in allowing the event to come into his life. Then too perhaps the changing of mental attitudes in the client's family or business could also change the time element; sometimes it could even wipe out the results of the prediction or change it to something else.

This is the difference between the psychic predictions and those of the ECK-Vidya, which is only the reading of the past, present and future records.

CHAPTER 5

THE ECK-VIDYA THEORY OF TIME-TWINS

The theory of time-twins is as old as the dawn of human history, yet the early ECK Masters who were the first to begin the use of the ECK-Vidya never spoke much about this aspect of the way of life. However, it grew in time because so many people were apt to believe in it as the theory of Soul-mates. It sprung up somewhat as legend or among the witchcraft cult during the Middle Ages and became popular. Today it is one of the stronger theories which many people want to believe.

In the beginning I would like to point out that there is little foundation for the Soul-mates theory. Many people desire to believe this as an excuse because of unhappiness and loneliness in marriages or because they have failed in a union with the opposite sex, or that they have never married. The justification which these people give have little basis in the worlds of the spiritual universe.

Of course there is an affinity between certain bodies because of the chemistry between them which brings them together. They can live together as man and wife much easier because there is less friction. But this is true of minerals, metals, plants, flowers and animals. Any chela who is a good student of the other worlds and who has developed an insight into the invisible planes will know that the lines of affinity are well established between people, and the things as named here. He will also know that many people will have affinity because of their past lives.

Yet what many who try to follow the path of occultism do not know is that the like aberrations within certain people will draw them together. Hatred is the greatest of these. Two people who have a great hatred for something can be drawn together and live in a degree of harmony which appears to others to be a constant conflict between them. Some can be drawn together when one appears to have no love at all for the other mate, yet they stay together in marriage throughout their natural lives and never seem to have any more differences than usual married couples.

I once knew of a young woman who died just a few days before her marriage to a very fine man. Her sister gave birth to a daughter, several years after the tragic death, and a strange pattern of behavior began to show in the daughter soon as she was able to walk and talk properly. Her intensity for playing the part of a mother, was greater than in the usual case of young girls. As she grew up her desire for marriage became a problem; it took on almost a neurotic behavior pattern. At times from childhood she would never answer to her own name but to the nicknames that her aunt, who died, was given. She even scolded others who tried to call her by any other name but this, and grew up answering only to the nickname of her aunt, which she retains to this day.

Her first dates in college turned out to be a disaster because all she could think about was marriage. Her present husband finally came onto the scene and she knew this was the affinity which was hers several years before when living in the body of the Aunt, and who had missed happiness through marriage. Their marriage has been successful with a large family and all the normal things which go with this sort of life. The husband recognized from the beginning what had happened and took it for what it was worth.

However, the Time-Twins theory is not considered strongly in the works of ECKANKAR, simply because we are dealing with lines of affinity and not the true spiritual meeting of two Souls, who could fall in love with one another in the lower worlds region. We find that in an automobile accident which might be caused by unknown reasons for one car practically leaped across the line in the middle of the road, and crashed into another, is often caused by the affinity of metals within the frame or motor of both cars which must meet although it is in violence.

Sex affinity is often brought about in the same manner, that in two people whose body chemistry is alike, the inevitable takes place. Of course emotions and feelings have something to do with this, but too often it's the affinity of the chemistry which is alike in the male and female bodies which brings about the meeting of the two, whether it's in insects, birds or polar bears.

Astrology tries to match up man and woman best according to their signs. While this is true, to a certain extent, I do find it not complete in its statements. One does have the knowledge to know that two people who have the same corresponding Zodiac signs which look for alike chemistry of bodies in the same sign, are often disappointed if they go into marriage.

The truth of the matter is that sex aberrations are sometimes the cause of all these problems. No one can say that the signs in the Zodiac matches up people, male and female, when they are in some deep danger such as the concentration camps in Germany during World War II, where sex was unusually high among the prisoners, nor among the poor where it is greater than in normal conditions, or middle class families.

Gopal Das, now the guardian of the Shariyat-Ki-Sugmad, on the Astral plane, when living here on earth and teaching ECKANKAR in ancient city of Karahota, in what is now the Gobi Desert, said this about the Time-Twins theory, "This has never been a proven fact in the spiritual history of mankind. It is only the case of some of the ignorant who have wanted to believe this."

Gotta, one of the first ECK Masters in this world was among the foremost of the Ancient Order of Vairagi to bring out the idea that the Time-Twins theory was not practical; that it is Soul Itself which becomes the one-in-one and finally faces the SUGMAD in ITS perfection of glory.

Soul, as Yaubl Sacabi, the great ECK Master, who is at the head of the spiritual city of Agam Des, and who is reputed to be somewhat of a thousand years or more old, once said, is the combination of two forces as long as It has to live in the lower worlds, the ECK and the Kal, and when It reaches perfection It becomes the ECK. Therefore we find the Time-Twins theory only applies here. As Soul unfolds toward perfection through life after life in this world It seeks what the mortal man believe is Its Soul mate.

Frankly It is seeking Itself, the ECK, on the positive side. It is not until Soul reaches the Atma Lok, the Fifth plane, that It discovers Itself as the ECK, and by becoming the ECK, It has attained the symbol of Its Soul mate. The two forces join and blend into one another; this means that the masculine and feminine forces within man are now one, and It cannot be anything but at oneness with Itself. Therefore It fulfills the theory of the Time-Twins, while at the same time the theory of union with God, as the philosophy of the Hindus teaches.

This is the noted union, or oneness with God. It is not what the

69

interpreted Hindu scriptures claim, but the union of the two forces within the individual Soul. Once it has happened the glory is significant, and Soul understands the symbolism of the Hindu claims. It becomes individualistic and cannot be anything, anymore than It is in Its own self, freedom and newly found strength. This is reality, and nothing more, nor anything less.

This is where the ECK-Vidya reading enters into accuracy, because it reads the true records of the true body of Soul, and none of the records of the other four bodies which are man's protective sheaths in the lower worlds. It reads all bodies if necessary but generally only that of the Atma Lok, the Fifth world of ECK.

The ECK-Vidya reader is not concerned with the Time-Twins theory, nor is he bothered with anything, but the reading of Soul in Its true state. If two people, man and woman, are born at the same time, on the same moment, anywhere in the world, it would not make them Time-Twins, or Soul mates, as occultism calls it. There are thousands, and perhaps even millions of people, men and women, born in this manner and it still doesn't apply to them as Time-Twins.

Rebazar Tarzs has said that unless one recognizes the fact that each Soul born within this world is a whole and fulfilled individual within himself he will struggle through life, being either a male or a female for the many centuries until one day he shall reach perfection and be neither as Soul.

Lai Tsi, the Chinese spiritual Master and one of the great ECK Masters now serving as the guardian of the Shariyat-Ki-Sugmad, the section on the Etheric plane, in the city of Arhirit, in the Temple of Golden Wisdom there, said that all persons should become aware of the male and female principles within themselves — the masculine and feminine which of course must be balanced before an individual Soul becomes perfected. This is the way into heaven, and the answer to the occult claims on Soul mates.

Therefore we find that the Time-Twins theory, or Soul mates is hardly anything more than an occult or psychic claim to get the individual thinking about mates, which isn't true because all of the spiritual qualities of man lie within himself, and is never split up into two component parts.

Those who give divination, or the prophecy-makers are not always filled with goodness for the human race. There are those who can be called the black prophets, or the evil ones who, like the dark magicians, are able to work out some sort of predictions concerning individuals at a price furnished by someone who desires revenge. This isn't unusual for there is often a battle of the exponents of divinations, the clairvoyants, mediums, mystics, psychics, spiritualists and astrologers.

It was during World War II that Karl Ernst Krafft, a native of Basel, Switzerland, and an investigator of occultism, witchcraft, astrology, and the psychic arts, made contact with the German Intelligence Department. He predicted the attempt on Hitler's life on November 7-10, which came true when somebody tried to bomb the Munich beer hall where Hitler made a speech and left early.

Although the German Government's official position was against the occult arts, Himmler who was in charge of the Intelligence Department, practiced the use of seers in his work. He promptly put an Austrian clairvoyant to work on the assassination attempt who came up with the right answers of who tried the bombing. The culprits were caught and tried for murder.

Almost immediately the rush was on to make everything look good for Hitler. His own astrologers began to come up with horoscopes that he would win the war. On the other hand the Allies had astrologers making charts on him which said the opposite. The German propaganda ministry even tried to fake Nostradamus' predictions of 300 years before to say that Hitler would be triumphant.

The British began to fake their own horoscopes on Hitler's defeat and smuggle them into Germany. Krafft's luck turned downward because of the Hess defection to England, for the German authorities believed he was linked with this disastrous affair for them. He died enroute to one of the prison camps.

The human animal resents change, and man grows older in his years, thinking little about his past. When he becomes elderly, generally his mind begins to revert to his childhood and youth. He thinks about his parents and those who were his companions during these years. It is the return to the past which only he can recall. Nobody else can recall these days but him. This is interesting for generally he has few people who will listen to his stories about his other days when life was sweeter. He wants to believe in a comfortable past and is afraid of the symbolic future of uncomfortable events. What has he to look forward to but old age, sickness and death?

It is extremely hard to give a reading for anyone who is elderly, except for an ECK-Vidya report. If the reader will be kind to the elderly person in his reading via the ECK-Vidya he can go into the future lives. He can give hope and happiness of the client's future life on some other plane; or he can tell him what is to come in his next life. This is far better than trying to read something out of a life which is nearing its end in this world. Any individual in this position should not ask for anything in his future except how to avoid sickness and unhappiness. Of course if there are special problems which come up such as relatives trying to move him into an old age home, or trying to get him to change his will, this makes for something solid for the ECK-Vidya reader to give positive answers.

Few persons if any will try to seek answers for themselves, but want them for someone else in their families. They are constantly seeking something outside, in the external world. The answer doesn't lie there, it lies within, and this is why the ECK-Vidya reading is so important.

There will be some who will argue with the ancient days of the ECK calendar. Already a few have said that the jewels which made up the symbolic meaning of each month in the olden times are wrong, but they cannot release themselves of the fact that they are still trying to go by astrology. Please remember that whatever anyone has learned in astrology doesn't go here in the ECK-Vidya. The mantic science of astrology is like so many of the so-called occult books appearing on the bookstands today; they are nothing but a farrago of nonsense from beginning to end. Others are so abstruse and difficult to understand that they bore the reader, while a third group contains some useful or even valuable information which is difficult to extract from pages of super-stitious trivialities.

Because very few people are able to separate their emotions from their mental power, it follows that the capacity to understand the msyteries of the true spiritual works, or even its fundamental teachings, is confined to a limited number of people. Those with spiritual power must use themselves as channels for the ECK, divorced from the mental and the emotional powers. Then they must learn to utilize the necessary emotions and mentality in such a way that they work by and through the ECK power. It is a combination of the psychic powers, trained and utilized, and put

72

into the right stream of the ECK power, which makes the perfect ECKist who can eventually learn to do the ECK-Vidya reading for others.

Everything within the individual begins in Soul. It uses thought as a creative power to reach the outer world. Emotions and feelings follow the thought power with good or bad effects according to whether the idea itself is constructive.

Actually the word good is not wholly apt, as a good thought can have its basis in a wrong emotion and so have a bad outcome. But a really constructive thought can never have a bad outcome as it builds rather than destroys. If it turns out to be a thought based upon a wrong emotion we might find the individual practicing black magic without him knowing it. Actually there are more people who practice black magic against themselves than ever directed at others. To tell one's self or to feel that he is inferior to others, or less clever or good looking, or to disparage himself in any way is negating the ECK power within himself, and this is black magic.

To think and act as if one is not only as good as others, but in some respects far better is white magic, for doing and setting it in motion will make it so. One responds to his own thoughts both consciously and unconsciously and so do others. Whether we believe it or not others react to our thoughts, spiritual power and psychic beliefs rather than to our words. Words never convinced anyone of anything against their will or influenced them to any extent. But a picked up thought or feeling does, and more people are natural telepaths than we realize.

Therefore, let us consider the months of the ECK-Vidya wheel and their workings with the law of karma, which will give an idea of how those born within different months can have influence on one another.

Astik, the first sign, which is the month of the emerald, within itself carries much of the negativeness of Niyamg, or the month of the onyx. There is not as much an indication of weakness as there is a constant effort to be strong, or an exaggeration of ambition. Astik is a rebellious period which is really against the restraint of Niyamg, the month of the onyx. Those born in this era of the Astik month are constantly struggling for perfection not realizing that the restraint and limitation of their own nature within themselves is the main problem. They can be easily depressed over almost anything.

73

The Astikean can mate somewhat with the Niyamgean with good results. Their chemistry is somewhat alike in nature as that which is between the emerald and the onyx stones. But again this is neither time-twins nor Soul mates as so many persons in the psychic field seem to think.

Those born during the month of Uturat, which is that of the bloodstone find themselves a follower of the path of Bhakti, or the path of love. Many persons who are within this era are great on the path of love, which eventually ends in God-Realization. Ambition to find that greatness in love which comes with the realization of God, sometimes comes to naught. The inordinate ambitions of all Uturatean people lies in their karmic background which makes each believe that he is somewhat greater than he is in his striving for perfection. Each one, rather most of those born in this period are notoriously unhappy for instead of gaining love as desired few find it. Mostly whatever they achieve is unsatisfactory, and they live and die in bondage to unfulfilled desires. Their linkup with the month of Hortar, the days of wealth is partly responsible for this because this can cause them to have a karma which is established with the month of the pearl. Yet those who do find happiness within this month of the bloodstone it is more often through spiritual unfoldment which brings them mates born in Hortar, month of the pearl. Again this is due to the chemistry of the two jewels and has nothing to do with the Soul mate theory.

Garvata which is the month of joy, or that of the jade, is truly a positive time. It is usually a strong intellectual person who is born under this sign, although it is sometimes influenced by the sign of Uturat with subjective emotional impulses. For one thing most people of this era are irritable and inconstant in their habits, and usually they are professional workers, sometimes writers, artists and those along the health lines such as doctors and dentists.

They have the ability to get along with those born in the sign of the jasper, or the month of Parinama. It is a bit of chemistry between the jewels which pulls them together better and closer than those of other months. You will find that the two are pretty close in their thinking, emotional feeling and happiness. Their work and ideas on religion, spirituality and careers somehow come together and have less irritation than other jewels.

Next is the days of hope or what we know as Ebkia, the sign of the opal. Those within this period are frequently victims of their own inadequate mental control which runs wild at times and undisciplined. As children nobody seems to have paid much attention to them because of their ability to know when to push hard and when to go easy on their whims.

The bad karma of the Ebkian works out through various reasoning powers of its own type. The spiritually undeveloped Ebkian develops the most extraordinary attitude on the numerous problems of their life and relationships with others. They are extremists in their likes and dislikes for their emotions form their thinking for them. If sympathetic they will go to any extreme end to help another; if it's a dislike they can breed furious unhappiness. Their mental existence becomes pretty scattered until they get under the hands of the living ECK Master.

The Ebkian gets along well with the Dzyanian, or the agate period. Both seem to have the same qualifications and are easier in feelings and thought with one another's company. This doesn't particularly mean that they have marriage ties better than other jewel months but could get along pretty good as life time partners should they care to work at it.

The people born during the days of truth, or month of the sapphire or what we know as Ralot, in the ECK-Vidya calendar, are very positive in nature. However those who are unbalanced in this period, frequently suffer from some form of obsession, a malady peculiar to the psychic nature of Mokshove, the month of the diamond. This obsession may range from a complex superiority in belief that they are the divine one sent here to save the world, to a very aggravated infallibility complex. The Ralot people often feel that they are not as other mortals, but of a peculiar pattern especially endowed with divine attributes. Their professions vary from evangelists, dictators, artists or financiers. They are natural born reformers and often driven to overwhelming impulses to change something of a social nature.

The aggressiveness in the nature of the Ralotist brings him together with those born under the sign of Mokshove, the month of the diamond. It is the hardness of the diamond which attracts the Ralotist.

Those who are born under the period of Sahak, or the moonstone are very fond of music. They are forced by conditions beyond their control to take leadership and responsibility which they do not want. They seek comfort, security and protection, but are seldom able to enjoy any of these. Taken away from their music everything becomes inharmonious and they cannot feel happy and secure. So many of the Sahakists are looking for something which isn't there with the individual. That is they are looking for happiness before they are spiritually unfolded and haven't reached the level in which the qualities of happiness and like characteristics are found.

Those born in this period are more likely to have an understanding with anyone who was birthed in the month of Kamitoc, or that of the ruby, the days of freedom.

Now for those who have been born in Kamitoc, the days of freedom, or the jewel of the ruby. These people are generally positive and regarded as the most artistic of the whole signs of the ECK-Vidya calendar. Its people are mercurial in nature, and frequently in revolt against limitations of society and family. Most of those from this period who have become successful have a very humble background as a child. Most of them become public figures because of their ability to manage people. Sometimes their bad karma limits their capacity to remain in high positions, and disaster will often follow the honors they receive.

As said in the above paragraph concerning those who were born in Sahak, the days of music or moonstones, the Kamitoc will be able to get along well with this sign. Marriage between the Sahakist and the Kamitoc will make a good match.

Next the period of Mokshove which is the month of the diamond makes for the days of light. It is a molder of men and women of strength, and those who get together as husband and wife during this period make a strong team throughout their lives in this world. The Mokshove's greatest problem is emotional control. The emotions of the ones from this era is that of the accumulated karma of other past lives. Where bad karma exists it causes truth to become involved in a thousand emotional reactions and loses much resemblance to integrity. Those born within this period often try to establish their own standards of honesty and conditions of life. It sometimes works especially if the individual is highly developed, and can lead to great attainment in the spiritual works, but too often in the less developed type, the judgement is hopelessly biased by the intensities of the emotions.

The Mokshove is able to get along quite well with the Ralotist, whose jewel is the sapphire. These two stones, the diamond and the sapphire are harmonious stones.

Those who have been fortunate to be born in the period of the Dzyani, or the month of the agate, and which is known as the days of friendship, are very highly moral people. They are entirely open and above board with their own thinking and emotions. It is a religious period in which those who turn to religion are very devoted and faithful to their cause. These people generally turn to science of some nature for their livelihoods, such as medicine, scientists, conservationists and occultism.

They have a karmic tie with people born in the period of Ebkia the month of the opal. This tie is not at all bad, and many of those who marry from these two periods find themselves in a greater harmony than if they had selected mates from another period. It appears that their karmic ties are somewhat similar and they have better help by adjusting to one another and getting rid of these karmas of each other through their married life.

The period of Parinama is that of the days of beauty, or month of the jasper. It is one of the strongest of the jeweled periods of the ECK-Vidya, as well as the most enduring. There is danger of introversion in this sign for the negative qualities of this era can turn back all negative emotions upon themselves and make difficult all mental, emotional and physical expressions. The Parinama is an independent, ambitious and progressive type of individual but his normal expression is almost impossible because of his peculiarly, crystallized personality. This often causes him to have problems in trying to spiritually unfold under the living ECK Master.

Because of his need to have moderation in his daily life he can find greater happiness with those born in the period of Garvata, the month of joy, or that of the jade. Such friends or mates can help the Parinama to overcome impatience, and to settle down to an appreciation of reasonable and simple things. Those under the sign of Parinama are often unhappy, not so much from the negatives of their state, but from the comparison of their position at the time, and the spiritual standards toward which their ambitions may be pointed.

Those born in the period of Hortar, the days of wealth, or month of the pearl, have a very positive attitude and also a peculiar fixed point of view. These people are generally liberals and will work on anything from social reforms to dietetics. The Hortarian is apt to be trying to sell something new to his fellowmen and taking away the disadvantage of that which they do not like. But these are original and capable people and have strong psychic influences over others. They are always in revolt against conservatism and the establishment. Likewise they are melancholy people and not easily cheered up unless they find something to change. Their karma is that of isolation and unhappiness in their environment.

The Hortarians are well mated with the Uturat because of the latter's ways of loving people. It is only the Uturatean who seems to have much influence on these people born in the gloomy, cloudy days of Hortar, the period of wealth.

Niyamg, or the days of charity, which is the month of the onyx, is the last of the twelve periods of the ancient ECK-Vidya calendar. Those persons born in this period are usually of a negative nature until the living ECK Master can have an opportunity to change them. They have specific karmic problems in wasting energy, because few persons born during this period know how to relax. This waste is often reflected in their actions and reactions to others. It is that period in which the cycle of the ECK-Vidya is completed and the living ECK Master is gathering up the loose ends of incarnations which the individual born in this period has gone through. Sometimes it is a heavy load of karma for the individual, but when it is paid, the incarnating Soul is then ready to step out fresh with this karma sublimated in spiritual power. Then he doesn't have to return to this physical universe ever again.

The Niyamg is fortunate to be able to get along well with those born in the Astik period, the month of the emerald. Because of the general wisdom of the Astikist if married they have a mate to help guide them through all the difficulties of this heavy karma while the living ECK Master is assisting in lifting it.

This is generally the way that the Soul mates theory got started, because certain signs had affinity between those born in respective periods of the ECK calendar. But as said before in the above paragraphs it is only a theory and not practical under any human circumstances.

The problems which the ECK-Vidya reader seeks to solve are understood to take place under three parts. These are: First, the place of Soul in Its own pattern of karma, which has caused the physical incarnation of Soul here on earth in Its present state.

Secondly, the level or plane of consciousness in which the Soul functioned prior to Its present life, which contributes the moral force to the present existence.

Third, is such detail and circumstances of the previous existence as may account for the karma, or progresses of retribution, which are at work in the present existence.

In addition to these, an ECK-Vidya reading could be erected for the time, rather that is the moment of death, for any individual by which the future state of the respective Souls of those who have this sort of reading is estimated, and established as to what plane they would be working upon after death of the physical body.

This part of the ECK-Vidya is concerned with that which we know was the larger part of life's action for the individual, and that which we live in at the present is only a fragment of this overall picture. To all those who know something of the philosophy of life and the works of ECK, man's present condition and state is but the result of his previous lives and actions. To understand this, is to discover the causes and conditions of one's present life, and often what his future lives might be.

Once in visiting the Katsupari Monastery in northern Tibet, which is under the ECK Master Fubbi Quantz, I found a painting on a ceiling which was called the Bhava Chakra, the cycle of transmigratory existence. This meant the cycles which Soul goes through while on this earth. The outer circle of this wheel was divided into twelve parts which are the periods of the jewels, and which were called nidanas, or the causes that move each individual Soul to reincarnate. These nidanas are the twelve ECK-Vidya signs, each of which contains within it an impulse to action, or a cause that brings Soul back again into this world.

The first nidana, under Astik, is represented by the unconscious will. This is called the blind man, and signifies Soul passing from death to rebirth, and on to death and rebirth again. The cycle of transmigratory existence.

The second nidana, under Uturat, is called conformation, and is represented by the potter and his pots, signifying Soul shaping Its materials of the mental and physical natures for this world.

The third nidana, under Garvata, is called the conscious will. It is typified by the restlessness of the human consciousness, or that of the money, and signifies the rise of conscious experience in the individual Soul of man.

The fourth nidana, under Ebkia, is that which we know as the self-consciousness, and is represented by a ship containing all that Noah's Ark had, man, woman, and animals. It signifies the rise of the quality of individuality.

The fifth nidana, under Ralot, is given in the symbol of an empty house. It represents the development of the sensory perceptions.

The sixth nidana, under Sahak, is that of a figure representing marriage, and it signifies the focusing of the sense perceptions upon the exterior objects.

The seventh nidana, under Kamitoc, is represented by a figure with an arrow through its heart. This signifies the illusion of pain and pleasure and their reaction upon Soul. To see through this illusion is to have freedom.

The eighth nidana, under Mokshove, is called desire. It is represented by a figure crawling in the dust with its hands up pleading to the heavens for its desires to be fulfilled. It signifies the experiences of gratification.

The ninth nidana, under Dzyani, is known as indulgence, and is represented by a man with food all around him, and stuffing himself with it. This signifies attachment to worldly possessions, and those who cannot give up such possessions.

The tenth nidana, under Parinama, is represented by maturity, and it signifies the fullness of material existence brought to its highest philosophical level.

The eleventh nidana, under Hortar is known as compensation. This sign is represented by the birth of a son. It signifies the paying of all debts to nature and final detachment from this physical world and its attachments.

The twelfth nidana, under Niyamg, shows the dead body being carried to the grave by twelve pall bearers. It signifies decay of all points of contact by which life is held to the material state, and spiritual unfoldment into the next world.

After the twelfth nidana, the first cycle for some begins again, and goes through all the cycles of existence. The nidana, of course, represents the dominating consciousness or the place of Soul in the great cycle of progress. While the ego has its birth, growth, maturity and decay, so many hundreds of these lives form together a greater cycle involving a vast progress of life moving through its many spiritual stages.

The nidana is determined by the ascendancy of Soul on the spiritual ladder to God. Thus a person born in Niyamg is born to the experience of detachment, for he is bringing a cycle of experience to an end. A person who is born in the period of Mokshove has the sole purpose of his existence to experience the consequences of greed, personality, and possession.

The ascendancy of Soul in the ECK-Vidya circle of life represents a minor cycle of experience within a greater one. This greater cycle is of course the twelve year cycle of which I have already spoken about. It qualifies and specializes the general significance of Soul's purpose in this world. For example, the fifth nidana, or Ralot is the outer manifestation of the sensory powers. This is usually manifested as ambition. As Soul progresses through the third nidana or Garvata, it represents the effort to establish individual sufficiency, and denotes that the ambitions will be of an intellectual or mental nature.

By calculations based upon this sort of arrangement, the primary purpose of Soul's incarnation is established to reach perfection and eventually God-Realization, then to serve somewhere in the universes as a co-worker with God.

CHAPTER 6

THE LIFE CYCLES OF MEN,
NATIONS AND PLANETS

The life cycles of men, nations and planets are strikingly different in a sense than one has ever believed, according to the ECK-Vidya. These cycles are natural and having been established centuries ago, since the beginning of time in this universe, it appears that man has either forgotten them or has given them up for something which he has felt to be more likely to fit his times in a less complicated manner.

When man began to put his confidence in other means of communication such as prophets, omens, augery, and oracles to name a few he lost the ability to communicate directly with the Atma Lok (Soul plane). For example, during August in the year of 333 B.C., Alexander the Great visited the Oracle of Ammon in western Egypt. He was plagued with anxieties and doubts about his destiny in the history of mankind. He had finished his campaign in Egypt and that country was now under his rule. Should he turn to the East and conquer the Persians as Philip, his father wanted to do but whose untimely death had cut short this ambition?

He was met and escorted to the oracle by Kita Sorgi, the great ECK Master of the day, where he listened to what the oracle had to say. The message which came out of the oracle was "He who destroys the East, shall in turn be destroyed by the gods." He asked Kita Sorgi what this meant but received no answer, because the ancient Masters of ECKANKAR do not often give replies of this kind, for it could upset the scheme of karmic patterns and reverse the whole trend of man's history on earth.

However, Alexander believed that ˜this meant that if he destroyed the political structure of the nations which he would conquer the prophecy would come true. Otherwise if he left the governments as they were, with some of his own army officers in charge as advisers, as well as promoting marriage between his troops and the local women of the country all would be well. He did all this, was known as a wise administrator and was popular in every country, including Persia, but through his strong will and personality he changed so much of the traditions and customs of the country that the plague of the gods, malaria, struck him down at the age of thirty-three.

The evolution of man began millions of years ago. It was during these early years that the Ancient Order of the Vairagi, the ECK Masters, learned there was a rhythm of life cycles, which had great influence on mankind. There were first the monthly cycles which were named after the various jewels, followed by the three year period or cycle called the Eceuques, or better known as the Triad which is of course much easier to pronounce. This consisted of a theory that man changes somewhat in his nature and bodily chemistry every three years. There would be thirty-six periods within this cycle that is made up of the varied metals and their influences on man. It is three into three, into three, or better known as the Triad in which the metals rule over the jewels of the thirty day periods, known otherwise as months.

These metals are Aluminum, Silver, Copper, Gold, Iron, Lead, Tin, Zinc and Mercury. These are the nine metals which rule over the sequence of the three in three, in three. They are known for their qualities which have life giving qualities for those living in the human consciousness state within the worlds of matter.

First, Aluminum, which is used so much as an amulet in the East with the desire to promote one's welfare, good fortune and happiness with material things. This is a progressive period of life.

Second is Silver, which is the period of quiet, moody times, mystical in its moonlike quality. It is passive in nature, feminine, and secretive. In amulets it is used for the keeping and protection of secrets. It is also a guard from the perils of water. Attuned to the sign of Niyamg, month of the onyx, silver is the metal of secret dreams and equally secret fears which brings it within the realm of moody attitudes which run from the highest to the lowest.

Copper is a metal much influenced by Garvata, month of the jade. It has the earth qualities of warmth and good food. The words glowing warmth would fit its descriptive qualities very well. Copper bracelets or having a piece of copper on one's own person has always been a guard against arthritis and rheumatism, both of which are aggravated by cold. All muscular discomforts caused by cold are also relieved by copper. Its vibrations so often counteract the effects of negative or depressive tensions set up by problems or lack of communication between people. The cheerful qualities of copper pans and pots in a kitchen so many times help keep down tensions and troubles within a household.

Gold is a fiery, dry metal. It is said to be the king of metals, and of course the metal of kings for all rulers of nations have made gold a standard of royalty. It is a heat intense metal, which symbolizes success in everything. It is the ruling metal of Kamitoc, month of the ruby. It is allied to those of royalty, the theatre and business. It seems to have been and will always be the metal which lures those brave enough, and strong enough to steal, murder or create wars over it.

Iron is a conductor of heat, but not the fiery, glowing kind that gold possesses. But it represents the terrible fury of battle, lust and gore. Iron is the metal for war machines, killing and the weapons that kill. It is a vengeful weapon. The Hittites of the ancient world were the first to find that iron was useful for conquest and set out to put all others in the Middle East under their power. The chains that hold man captive and are resistive of liberty are made of iron. Even when its uses are beneficial like instruments for heating, the iron contains the fury of the inner furnace; there is a wall of glowing metal between the fire and the world.

Lead has always been a serious, somber metal with a heaviness which rather depressed those who had anything to do with it. However the heavy-spirited manner in which it is encased does not prevent it from being mystically endowed. It is used by the Germans who are not a light-hearted people anyway, to foretell the future on New Year's day. This form of divination is called Blieigiessen, and is given in the following manner: a small amount of lead is dissolved in a spoon over a candle and when it is liquid, it is dropped in a bowl of cold water. The shape that it forms is supposed to foretell the year ahead for the person holding the spoon. The shape is interpreted as representative of the events of the year ahead, with the idea that the form points to some specific event in the twelve months' period.

Tin is somewhat associated with Hortar, the month of the pearl. It is symbolic of good fortune and a metal of progress and development. On the psychic planes it is a metal which is moist and warm and therefore an expanding force.

Zinc is a metal which is in harmony with Dzyani, the month of the agate, the days of friendship. It is a metal which attracts those who are rather dry-witted in manner and is a conductor of deep loyalty in the human nature. It is one which has been known for several thousands of years, somewhat heavy in nature, yet able to serve the purpose of being an all purpose metal, known in the ancient times and used by the Romans. It is greyish in color and used a great deal in the ancient and middle ages for making of household wear, dishes and cups. Today it is one of the best alloys that we have in the making of many different types of things.

It is also connected with Ralot, the month of the Sapphire, and has a deep mystical meaning for those interested in what influence that it may have on their life. It can be worn, as pure zinc, in an amulet for warding off lung troubles and stomach upsets. The only place that it might be possible to get pure zinc amulets is through special shops which sell occult materials.

Mercury is the last of the three in three, in three metals. It is influenced by the month of Uturat, that of the bloodstone. Those who are most influenced by this metal find that it represents love and freedom in their lives, yet they are of a fluid nature because of the aspects of the metal. It is a metallic element, yet it is liquid at ordinary temperatures. Because of its mobility and its color it was first called quicksilver by the alchemists about the 6th century. It was known to the ancient Chinese and Hindus at least 2000 years B.C. Also it was found in the tombs of the Egyptian rulers of 1500 B.C.

As stated those who are influenced by the metal are free in their ideas of love and freedom. But on the other hand these people usually have a mercurial disposition; they can run from hot to cold in their moods on an instant's notice. Friends are usually sensitive in their presence because of this quick change in disposition.

The Eceuques, or the Triad makes the mental change in man, every three years. He becomes more alert in his thinking provided that he is unfolding spiritually according to the way of ECKANKAR. Otherwise if a person is not unfolding in the right manner, or going backwards, the Triad is likely to work in reverse. That is should the individual be idle in thought, or shiftless in his mental processes. But once the individual turns to trying to improve himself mentally there is little problem in his gaining in intellect and understanding of all things through the mental senses.

The yearly period is the little cycle, the three year period is the middle cycle and the twelve year period is the greater cycle. This latter period is taken up for study in a brief way at this time.

The greater cycle which is called the Haram, or the Duodenary, is the higher vibrations which rotate every twelfth year and changes the chemistry and spiritual makeup of men, nations, planets and communities, by uplifting those Souls which make up these units of civilizations. Of course some will not be lifted because of their degeneration or slow progress anyway.

The years within the Duodenary cycle have each been given a name by the ancients which have a bearing upon the seasons, elements, plants and some form of nature. These are repeated again here for the benefit of the reader: The first cycle is called the Cycle or Years of the Fierce Winds. The second cycle is the Cycle of the Bright Snows. The third is the Cycle of the Brilliant Sun. The fourth is the Cycle of the Beautiful Flowers. The fifth is the Cycle of Full Moon. The sixth is the Cycle of the Strange Storms. Seventh is the Cycle of the Wandering Seas. Eighth is the Cycle of the Bountiful Earth. Ninth is the Cycle of the Abundant Fruits. Tenth is the Cycle of the Raging Fires. Eleventh, the Cycle of the Lavish Grains, and twelfth, the Cycle of the Trembling Leaf.

These cycles blend with one another, each turning a wheel which brings about the downfall or the building of a nation, community or new world within the universe. Like the universal Zodiac, the ECK wheel also has twelve signs, or divisions, as just given. These signs instead of lasting approximately thirty days, the periods of the ECK wheel last twelve years. Each year is named from some function of nature, and it is believed that people born during the cycle of that element or nature are endowed with qualities and tendencies inherent to the sign.

The cycles within one's life can be worked out from the time of his birth. This will give you an idea of what cycle that you are in today. For example if you were born in 1924, you would just be entering the fourth cycle, that of the Beautiful Flowers. Or if born in the year of 1900, you would be entering the cycle of the Strange Storms. Nations born in certain eras, for example the United States was founded July 4, 1776. It means that we have gone through approximately 15 full cycles, therefore this country would be in the cycle of the Brilliant Sun again. This is true for the United States is standing at the peak of its wondrous wealth and spiritual heights.

This can easily be worked out by just figuring out the date of the birth of a nation, city, or country, subtracting the present day from the birth and dividing by twelve. Then go back through the cycles and see just where the exact cycle is standing at the present time. The characteristics of the nations, communities, or the individual are somewhat alike in nature. These are as follows according to each individual cycle.

The first cycle which is known as the Thigala, or the Years of the Fierce Winds is a feminine period. This signifies that the individual who was born during this period has the tendency to get what he wants by waiting and manipulating, by designing and personal attraction, rather than making a struggle in an open and active manner.

Within the masculine principle in this first cycle we find that any man so born as a son of the fierce winds, his traits will be subtle, not overbearing, and obvious. He will show strength in a quiet way, rather than with noise and bluster. Even though this is true, he should never allow others to push him, or bully him. His natural consideration to be too considerate of others' feelings will get in his way.

Those born in the Cycle of the Fierce Winds should be very careful with their health. They need a strong diet of proteins and vegetables, and should be careful not to get too many carbohydrates in their intake of foods.

Also there is something of the inevitable about the life and thought of these people. They are seldom defeated because they do not recognize defeat.

The second cycle which is known as the Ginthe, or the Years of the Bright Snows, is a masculine, or active sign. Those born in this period are generally aggressive. They have the determination to go after what they want with roars of determination. Often they are ruthless if anyone stands in the path of their ambitions.

The women born in the Years of the Bright Snows almost always get the men they want. They will even remake themselves into the image of the kind of woman their man desires, in order to bring him into marriage and under their influence. But they do make good mothers and housekeepers for their family.

The men born under this sign are almost assured success in any field they enter for careers and employment. With the right

THE ECK-VIDYA WHEEL

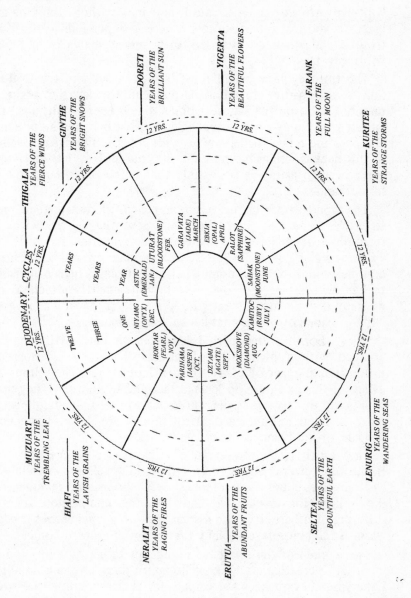

THIGALA — YEARS OF THE FIERCE WINDS

GINTHE — YEARS OF THE BRIGHT SNOWS

DORETI — YEARS OF THE BRILLIANT SUN

YIGERTA — YEARS OF THE BEAUTIFUL FLOWERS

FARANK — YEARS OF THE FULL MOON

KURITEE — YEARS OF THE STRANGE STORMS

LENURIG — YEARS OF THE WANDERING SEAS

SELTEA — YEARS OF THE BOUNTIFUL EARTH

ERUTUA — YEARS OF THE ABUNDANT FRUITS

NERALIT — YEARS OF THE RAGING FIRES

HIAFI — YEARS OF THE LAVISH GRAINS

MUZUART — YEARS OF THE TREMBLING LEAF

DUODENARY . . . CYCLES

ONE YEAR

THREE YEARS

TWELVE YEARS

12 YRS.

ASTIC (EMERALD) JAN./UTURAT (BLOODSTONE) FEB.

GARAVATA (JADE) MARCH

EBKIA (OPAL) APRIL

RALOT (SAPPHIRE) MAY

SAHAK (MOONSTONE) JUNE

KAMITOC (RUBY) JULY

MOKSHOVE (DIAMOND) AUG.

DZYAMI (AGATE) SEPT.

PARINAMA (JASPER) OCT.

HORTAR (PEARL) NOV.

NIYAMG (ONYX) DEC.

intelligence in practically any endeavor they are successful, but failure comes too often because this type people so many times will leap into movements, causes and jobs without thinking and create havoc instead of success. There is a possibility of serious trouble and divorces provided they marry mates born in the Ginthe cycle.

The third cycle is called the Doreti, the cycle of the Brilliant Sun. It is a positive era and its natives seem to reach the heights of material and spiritual success under the proper conditions. The Doreti who follows his natural talents often becomes a politician. He loves the power which comes with politics, and natural leaders in this field as well as business and the church. If he lets his hunger for power go astray it is possible that he becomes dangerous to himself and society.

The women born in this period appear to dominate their men, to such an extent that they may lose them by divorce or separation or plainly drive them to self-destruction. A Doreti woman will often deliberately pick a man for a mate who is complex and difficult to dominate simply because he is a challenge to her own nature. But once she becomes deeply attached, and does not lose the attachment with him easily, she will make a good wife, provided of course that he is the right man.

Those born in this period have such a hard-driving nature, coupled with a high ratio of success that they often arouse jealously and anger of their associates and friends. They should be aware of this and develop instead tact and diplomacy. They mate well with the passive signs, those who have understanding and grasp of their nature, particularly those born in the first cycle, Thigala, or the Years of the Fierce Winds.

The fourth cycle is that called Yigerta, or the Years of the Beautiful Flowers. Those born within this cycle are usually shy and sensitive, under the feminine sign. The individual generally has the ability to understand, and feel the compassion for the suffering of others. It is also associated with a craving for security, warmth and comfort, especially that of a well-ordered home.

The women of this sign have a tendency to marry young and be involved in creating a well kept home for themselves and families. Otherwise they make good careers for themselves in social work and as doctors, or nurses. They have a natural talent in caring for the sick, aged and afflicted. These women have a shy, retiring charm which makes them very attractive to men.

The male Yigerta too often suffers because he is too sensitive to personal slights. He has a tendency to withdraw, instead of fighting back, or shrugging things off. However, in his own sensitive way he makes many friends, and can go farther in the business or professional world than some who are irritable and unfeeling. They will marry well provided their mates are of the signs of the Wandering Seas and Raging Fires.

The fifth cycle is the Farank, or the Years of the Full Moon. These persons born during this period are usually indirect and subtle, but honest and good natured with sharp, but witty minds. Although this is a positive sign, the aggression in these persons is quiet and tactful. For example the female born of this era is of gentle nature from all appearance and exceedingly seductive. She knows what she wants and is capable of twisting everything to suit herself, with her man, and can win him over with clever, subtle ways to gain her points and what she wants. She must beware of getting involved with a man of outstanding forthright nature who could get annoyed by her wits and wiles, failing to understand her nature, which is sincere and well-intended for the whole of things within her sphere of being.

The male Farank has the tendency to plot and scheme to increase his ambitions. If he controls this trait in himself, or uses it for the better of all concerned, there is no reason why he cannot fulfill his ambitions.

These people do well to marry with their own cycle for they understand one another better than those from the other cycles. Otherwise marriage with the Cycle of Bountiful Earth, the eighth, is a good one, but never should there be marriages fulfilled with those of the ninth or twelfth cycles.

The sixth cycle is known as the Kuritee, or the Years of the Strange Storms. These persons born during this cycle are definitely under a positive sign. They have strong tendencies toward strength, vigor and endurance and accept the burdens and responsibilities of life, even without complaint in some of the worst situations. They are also basically happy and healthy people, and usually have a love of nature and the open air.

The females born under this sign are open and frank with most people, but more so upon meeting the man of her choice. Once she finds a man of her choice she can usually adapt to whatever way of life he chooses and maintain her integrity and pride as a person. She must however pay attention to her dress and grooming.

The men born in this cycle usually have great success with women. He should remember that it will be a tragedy if he should keep changing women; although he can have lots of girl friends, he is most happy when he has settled down and is leading a life of quiet domesticity.

These people should avoid marriage with those of the Seltea persons, those of the eighth cycle, that of the Bountiful Earth. These are two cycles which seem to infuriate one another. On the other hand they can mate well with the seventh cycle that of the Wandering Seas, and the ninth, the cycle of the Abundant Fruit.

The seventh cycle is the Lenurig period, which is the Years of Wandering Seas. This is a negative sign associated with the love of tradition, a respect for authority, and a concern for good manners and decorum. Such traits lead to the Lenurigs being quiet and cautious. They usually make better followers than leaders, but are solid citizens and prudent in their decisions in their daily lives.

The male in this cycle is overlooked quite often by his superiors when the chance for advancement arises. Unless he makes the effort to make himself noticed, his very many valuable qualities will simply go unnoticed, and his good judgement overlooked.

The female Lenurig usually does quite well in the business world because of her solid, slow-moving but wise actions which offset the playful attitude often associated with other women. She excels as a wife and mother because her temper is slow to be stirred, and she is endlessly patient with her family. This type is found dominant in the middle European women, as most of these races, especially the Germanic race comes under this cycle.

These people do well in marriage with those in the sixth cycle, which is the Years of the Strange Storms, and the tenth cycle, the Years of the Raging Fires. They should not be connected in marriage with those who were born in the second cycle, the Years of the Bright Snows, nor the third cycle, the Years of the Brilliant Sun. The latter cycles are not in harmony as much as the first two with those born in this era, the seventh cycle, the Lenurig.

The eighth cycle, that which is called Seltea, is the Years of the Bountiful Earth. It is a dualistic period, being both the masculine and feminine and this leads to the complication and often contradictory nature shared by those born in this era. These people are generally quick-witted, but often slow to learn. They are good natured, but when angered can be vicious. They are fickle, but once attached to someone or something they remain loyal for a long time, perhaps as in marriage till death do them part.

The female of this period is inclined to flirt, and should be careful that she does not carry this too far or it will be dangerous for her. She has the talents and traits to do many highly and splendid things with fashion design, interior decorating and related fields, because her sense of color is strong.

The male Seltea, too, often excels in the field of arts. He can be extremely successful in the intellectual fields, such as teaching and science. But his dualistic nature often makes it difficult for others to understand him, and thus sometimes frustrates his ambitions at least temporarily. This makes him a hard person to live with, but if he can pick his mate well, she will be one with lots of patience and understanding of his temperament.

These people do well to marry those born in the fifth cycle, the Years of the Full Moon. They should avoid those born in the sixth cycle, the Years of the Strange Storms, in most cases, for their solid natures do not fit well with these complicated traits of the Selteas.

The ninth cycle is known as the Erutua, or the Years of the Abundant Fruits. The Erutuaians are fundamentally tough people, who have a real, hard positive attitude on life, and hardly anything ever gets them down. They tend to be tough, determined and dynamic people. They fight for what they want so long and hard that they usually get it. But many times they make real enemies by stepping on other people as they make their way up the ladder of success in this material life.

The female Erutuaian is usually a very highly charged sexed person. She certainly enjoys male companionship, and is likely to get very unhappy provided she does not get attention, nor what she wants out of a man. But because of her essential femininity she would like to be dominated by her man, yet her inborn streak of toughness often outweighs this feminine trait, and creates problems within herself and her man.

The male in this period is a powerhouse of ideas and ambitions. He will work around the clock in order to make a success of things, and usually enjoys it. He can do without sleep where others cannot, he enjoys being with women whom he can dominate but it is seldom that any woman can ever dominate him.

The Erutuaians and those born in the sixth cycle, the Years of the Strange Storms get along well even in marriage. Those from the fourth cycle, the Years of the Beautiful Flowers also get along well but they cannot get along with those born in the fifth cycle, the Years of the Full Moon.

The tenth cycle is that called Neralit, or the Years of the Raging Fires. The persons born in this period are somewhat feminine in nature and make excellent friends. They are honest, sincere and mostly trustworthy. They usually have placid and untroubled dispositions, and this sort of trait runs all through their lives from birth to death. That is unless they come into contact with those born in the ninth cycle, the Years of the Abundant Fruits. These two signs cannot come to any agreement on many things. Also those in the twelfth sign, the Cycle of the Trembling Leaf, will bring about a similar problem between the two.

The female Neralit is a person to be cherished as a wife, for she is deeply devoted in her loyalty to her husband and the care of her children. She will do most anything including work and will even fight for the happiness of her family and those that she cares for during her lifetime. Neither will she ever forget a friend.

The man born in this period has the characteristic traits of being trustworthy to a fault, occasionally running into some trouble although not seriously when considered. But he is often taken advantage of because of his basic faith in people and their goodness, in which he has a firm belief. On the other hand he is apt to have many friends, who will come to his aid in the time of trouble and need.

These people do well to marry those who are of the third cycle, the Years of the Brilliant Sun. Their qualities should complement each other, but most of all they should avoid those of the twelfth cycle, the Years of the Trembling Leaf.

The eleventh cycle is that which is called Hiafi, or the Years of the Lavish Grains. These people born in this period are very orderly, and their very nature is that they are slow to arouse any emotion, especially anger. But whenever they do such anger becomes fierce and unforgiving when aroused. They take a long time to grasp an idea, but when it happens they will delve to the very depths to learn every possibility about it, and its related fields.

The women who are natives of this cycle are too often overlooked by men because of their quiet, slow nature. But the man who discovers what she really is will find that she has a depth of feeling and understanding which is rare of women in other cycles.

At the same time the men who are born in the eleventh cycle are apt to be highly successful in research and other related fields which have the need of patience and long periods of slow progress to find something which is worthwhile to mankind. They are also quite philosophical about life, and stoical in their attitude toward pain and the usual disappointments in life. But they should pay attention to their health for this is apt to be one of their weaknesses in life.

They do well in marriage to those in the seventh and tenth cycles, which are respectively: the Cycle of the Wandering Seas, and the Cycle of the Raging Fires. They could have a stimulating marriage with those born in the eighth cycle, the Years of the Bountiful Earth, however it often turns out to be so turbulent that it leads to disaster, and resolving of marriage.

The twelfth cycle is that called the Muzuart, the Years of the Trembling Leaf. These people are hyperactive and cheerful in their disposition. But they tend to tire themselves to the point of sheer exhaustion because of their sheer excess of zeal for doing a good job. They do enjoy poking around in some odd corner of the world doing things that few people have ever done, and exploring the occult and the psychic sciences.

Some women born during this period have the knack of incessant chatter which drives mates, relatives and friends up the wall. Their enthusiasm for almost everything that appears in their lives is too much for others. Yet despite this most men will be and are highly stimulated by them, and often, as mates and employees find them irreplaceable. Women of this cycle do well in the entertainment world, and often in newspaper work.

The men born in this cycle are usually highly placed executives; they seemed to have a natural talent for this type of career. They are also good as explorers, detectives and reformers. Once they become interested in a subject they follow that subject as far as they can, often becoming so absorbed that they forget to eat or sleep. They sometimes have a tendency to put up a facade which will mask their real intentions and concern about their own problems, and how they feel about others.

These people do well in marriage with those in the first and third cycles, respectively, the Years of the Fierce Winds, and Years of the Brilliant Sun. However, they can do reasonably well with most any of those born in any cycle of the duodenary cycles.

In case it has been overlooked the names of these cycles are representative of the periods which the elements of nature have to go through each twelve years. During the early times on earth, that is in ancient days, cycles were far more prominent than they are today. For the first twelve years of the cycle the fierce winds blew constantly driving people into some shelter, caves or stone houses which would resist the winds. This was about fifty thousand years ago when man had very little to protect himself from the elements of the earth. So he called this period the Thigala, or the Years of the Fierce Winds. This occured high up in the Himalayan Mountains near what is now the northeast border of Tibet, and of course throughout the present site of the Gobi Desert and Mongolia.

When the heavy winds had died down snow began to fall and it fell for several years before halting. This was the cycle of Ginthe, or the Years of the Bright Snows. After halting the sun came out and its light gleamed upon the snows causing them to have a brightness and glitter which man had never seen before. During both periods the adepts of the Ancient Order of the Vairagi, the Masters of ECKANKAR, were busy helping people who had become destitute by these unusual phenomena of nature. Food had to be taken to the people, nursing care was needed for the sick, and many other things which gave them comfort and care.

Then the sun became brilliant and hot, after twelve years of snows, and the land turned into almost a tropical vegetation. This was the period called Doreti, the cycle of the Brilliant Sun.

Following this came a pleasant warm period for the next twelve years, which became Yigerta, the Years of the Beautiful Flowers, for flowers filled the land. The cycle shifted again and man found himself in a period of full moon every night. This was the Farank, or the Years of the Full Moon. When this ended another cycle began which was the Kuritee, or the Years of the Strange Storms which swept the earth driving man into heavy shelters again. Then came the Lenurig, the Cycle of the Wandering Seas, in which the land was drowned by the seas and many were drowned, while others took to the tops of the high mountains where they rebuilt their civilizations. The waters finally receded and man came off the mountain tops to the rich valleys where the earth was in bloom with all living things they needed. This was Seltea, the Years of the Bountiful Earth, in which man lived splendidly and was well kept, and soon forgot the ECK Masters, and the SUGMAD, the divine reality.

This period lasted twelve years of course, and then came the Erutua, the Years of the Abundant Fruits. For some strange reason which man has never figured out the next period was one of abundant fruits growing everywhere serving him with their sweetness and delight. He didn't know that the earth was tilting every twelve years so that life here was affected and these changes came about which had great results on him and his environment.

Following this period, there was a swing back into the negative or Kal period called Neralit, which was the Years of the Raging Fires. The volcanoes hidden deep within the earth became alive, and once again man had to flee his home to find shelter somewhere in safety. Millions died during this period of twelve years, but then when the fires died out there came the eleventh cycle which is called Hiafi, the Years of the Lavish Grains. Again man lived well giving up his worship of God in his desires to feed the body with grains and foods which were lavish during this time.

Then came the trembling of the earth, a strange phenomenon, which he could not understand, and stood in fear watching the trembling tree leaves which would warn him of a shaking earth. This was the Muzuart, the Years of the Trembling Leaf. It was a period when the earthquakes shook the world and caused upheavals and destructions everywhere. New mountain ranges were formed in India, which became the highest in the world; the Andes in South America became prominent, and the Rocky Mountains in the United States were formed.

When he found all the strange things happening and tried to hide from them, man only succeeded in making himself conspicuous. He appealed to the ECK Masters who gave him aid and comfort during these years, and finally brought everything to an end so that he, man, would once more become prodigious in his multiplying of the races and make the earth a better place to live.

If anyone would examine the history of the world, mankind and nations it will be found that underneath the glossy surface of civilizations these twelve cycles, which include twelve years within each, do exist. There should be 144 cycles in the life of each individual as there was in the old days, but today man has shortened his life through stress, strain and pollution. Now he lives just about half of what he is supposed to live.

CHAPTER 7

THE ECK-VIDYA INTERPRETATION OF DREAMS

The dream world is as much of the ECK-Vidya as it makes up the means of understanding life. The ECK sages of old were of the opinion that if one could understand the mystery of sleep, freedom would automatically come to them. Therefore in this chapter we are going to explore the realm of dreams and sleep. Also because it is related, we will thereby touch on the subject of visions.

Almost everyone asks why do all creatures sleep? We can also include in this plants and mineral life too, for it has been proven that even plants having consciousness will take a certain period of their day to spend in sleep. Since minerals and rocks too have a certain state of consciousness we can presume that they also sleep.

For the most part sleep is a habit, something that is certainly agreed upon as being necessary for survival. It isn't a fact that we could do without sleep, but rather point out that we most likely sleep too much. The average person sleeps longer than necessary because sleep is a very convenient method of escape from this world of reality. When the pressures of the day push in on him, and when stress becomes too unbearable, or when he loses interest in some form of expression, he is likely to desire sleep.

Science often makes claim that sleep is a carry-over from the cell memory, when at a certain stage of life experience, man slept because it was dark and convenient at the time for sleeping. But it's a well known factor that during the sleep process there is a rebalancing of chemicals, life forces, and a general readjusting. It's known that scientists have worked with a technique of directing a flow of radiation at a person who was tired and fatigued, and by neutralizing the fatigue toxins the individual is able to retire and gain from four hours of sleep that which would be as beneficial as eight hours. This made up for a theory that perhaps someday it would be possible to do away with sleep entirely. But not for all people; there are still those who will always be in that state of consciousness of trying to escape life.

It is only during sleep that most people will automatically link up with the healing and regulating currents of the universe. It is known that one day in the future, in the next century, man will be able to do this consciously and at will. We know that the ECK Masters, in the Ancient Order of the Vairagi, are able to live without sleep if necessary.

Army medical researchers have recently brought out that those who sleep only a few hours a night tend to be brighter and livelier doers than those who are long sleepers. The report from the army states that long sleepers are turned inward and are conflict conscious. The researchers tried to determine in their efforts the ratio between sleep and efficiency, in their study of one group of men who habitually needed no more than six hours of sleep and another group which customarily slept eight hours or longer. It was found that the short sleepers were active, outgoing men, flexible and sociable, relatively high on the social scale.

On the other hand it was found that those who were long sleepers tended to be more introverted and creative, but less successful at sustained work. Part of the reason why long sleepers sleep is that they have longer and more dreams than those needing less sleep. The more introverted people are more conflict conscious than very active people, and use the longer dream time to work on intrapsychic problems.

After 72 hours of sleep deprivation there were significant changes in all performance measures, with a marked loss of ability to concentrate and remain alert, the medical research team reported. However, I have seen Rebazar Tarzs and other great ECK Masters go without sleep for days because they live upon such a high level of expression, so in tune with the ECK, that they can operate in the body for practically 24 hours daily and never feel fatigue. Three or four hours of sleep seems to be all that is necessary for them. They live a full life, yet relaxed because they do not carry the burdens of mental and emotional strain, but have long learned to cast the burden into the ECK and rest in pure faith.

When any ECK chela is working with the ECK stream of power, there is little reason why the body will run down. Energy can flow through it steadily, and there will be few if any counter effects unless the Kal (negative) power gets in the way. When one resents their work, lives under great strain and stress, allows himself to worry and fear life, he causes a short circuit and the body runs down, gets out of tune and starts to malfunction.

Most people sleep one-third of one-half of their lives away. Trying to fight obstacles will not help any, but attunement with life brings victory. But they reach greater victory when the dream state is brought under control. Many persons dream vividly and in full color, with alive senses. Others dream in black and white, then only with a small amount of awareness. Some put importance on the nature of dreams and keep a daily log of them to see if there is some connection between the sleep dream and the awakened dream.

There is a connection between the dream state and the waking state, for often the dreaming is put together from the material taken in during the awakened state. Dreams are often part of the unconscious memories and need careful analysis and understanding. The literal interpretations of dreams are too often misleading for what the world of beyond is telling the sleeper has no parallel in this world.

There are many persons who have a pad of paper and pencil on the nightstand, and are able to awaken right after a dream to write it down. The next morning it could be found that certain questions were answered, or a problem solved in the dream state, and they could act upon it almost at once.

Anyone who has training can dream consciously for when he dreams and is conscious of the process, then he learns to see how this waking state is also a dream. Just as in the dream state any ECKist can learn to manipulate the environment, do anything he desires, simply by the knowledge that it can be done. Also in this waking dream state he can do the same, when he learns the techniques of doing it.

At night when he retires it must be accepted that he is going to dream consciously, or allow the ECK Dream Master to take over and see that he dreams of whatever is vital to his spiritual growth. It will likely not happen during the first few times but eventually as he drifts off to sleep with the expectancy of finding his own dream state to his liking, it will be found that he is conscious of the fact that he is dreaming.

He may be playing a role in a dream experience, or may be a silent witness as others enact their roles, much in the manner of watching people on a movie screen. After this one learns to change his dream at will, changing the events, moving at will from circumstance to circumstance. Then he learns to start, stop and go forward or backwards, just as he desires in learning that this is only a projection of his own mind and thoughts. He also learns to turn on sensation, make the dreams bright or dim, color or in black and white.

If anyone wants to learn to consciously move into a new or higher plane during his dream state, he must become conscious of this sort of state in the beginning. Then he anchors his attention on some solid object in his room or if this doesn't work tries putting it on something in the dream state. While he does this, he gives himself a command to awaken and as he anchors on to this object as a point of concentration, he will find himself rising as it were through veils of consciousness into a new plane, just as solid as the physical. If he should fail to maintain his concentration on an object in the dream, he would lose his connection and sink into a dream state and become awakened in a natural way.

This question always arises with the person who is trying to do this experiment. "What should I do if I am consciously dreaming, or in a different plane, and want to get back into the awareness of the physical body?" There is always the basic rule to follow: Assume with the sense of feeling that you are in your regular physical body, and this will be at once.

When the chela has had experience with this type exercise then he becomes a master of dimensional experience. The only reason that all people are in this particular, physical world is that they have agreed that it is the only solid and real one they know.

However, when anyone wants the experiences of dreaming of what is going to take place in his future he must take up a different approach. He must first realize that his future is set out ahead of him in accordance to his considerations and beliefs. When the seeker is able to change his present pattern of understanding and belief, he automatically alters the future sequence of his life.

Therefore we find that it is possible to dream, and while in that state, dream of future events; for events are always a reality of the present moment. We only experience them from various points of view and this gives the concept of time. It is possible to dream of events of the future, which are lodged in the deeper recesses of the mind, but only come about in some future awakened experience.

We soon learn through the ability to manage our dreams that those experiences in this state can be changed. If some dreams bring about fears and other unpleasant experiences, we do not have to accept them, by changing our outlook on them. This can be handled without difficulty even though one doesn't think of it being unusual. The living ECK Master is always standing by in case the chela fails in his attempt to make the change. If he is called upon it is then that he, the living ECK Master, steps into the life of the chela to help him change his dream state.

Some persons dream vividly, others hardly notice their dreams. Sleep and dream is normally the astral senses in action, although there are times in which the individual goes far beyond this into the true spiritual worlds. When awake man experiences through the physical senses, but when he dreams it is often through the astral senses. When one has dreamless sleep, it is through the causal or mental area of being. But when he has a deep, dreamless sleep it is closer to the pure states of heaven, in that of pure awareness, and if one awakens in this state he is apt to find himself in the true heavenly worlds.

In the field of visions it's found that men and women both have been able to have experiences of visions throughout all religious history. But the misunderstanding which comes with the layman's knowledge is that he believes that all visions are given by the Supreme Deity or by grace. Just as dreams are subconscious experiences, so visions are more on the superconscious level, though it is possible for them to become mixed on both levels. All visions are filtered through the conditioned consciousness of the individual, therefore partially colored by the belief of the individual.

Dreams or visions of relatives or friends who have translated from this world are not necessarily indicative of the return of that person, though we like to think it is true. Mortal longing or we should say loneliness is the reason why these dreams and visions come about. Perhaps many times we like to think that our visions and dreams are sent to us from God. This is the Kal speaking through the ego, but it certainly isn't truth. If you have that objective ability to understand visions and can separate such from hallucination, it could readily be seen that many persons who founded religions and sects were far from truth. These founders were unable to distinguish hallucination from truth, and in their own ignorance developed followers, who likewise believed their leader was given truth through visions.

There are religious records of individuals who have had certain types of phenomenon, of course, but this is really psychic and doesn't represent truth. Statues have come alive and spoken, tears have appeared on saints' faces and visions of the great saints or leaders of religions have come to certain people, thus creating new sects, religions and cults. We do not dispute this but it is one way that the Kal splits the followers of certain groups who are getting close to truth.

Very often a vision might come to the person in contemplation in symbolic form and will need interpretation. This happens because the individual is not opened enough in the spiritual consciousness to know truth. By knowing this you then find that many of the ancient prophets who had visions did not have the higher consciousness; they were in the state of the lower consciousness which must give visions to a participant in symbols. Truth filters through the human conditioning of consciousness and breaks upon the lower, or human state at that level of man's understanding. Few are blessed with the understanding of truth, others see visions, others have symbolic visions and many dream dreams.

Once you learn to dream consciously it will break the belief in limitation. If Soul wishes to bring out that part of Itself in knowledge and truth, because It is omnipresent, omniscient and omnipotent there is a way of giving help from the outer consciousness. When you go into sleep, relax and agree within that upon awakening you will have an answer to whatever it is you desire. Upon awakening it's found that it will be in the forefront of your thoughts. At the moment of slipping from sleep, or vice versa, there is a moment when you are opened to truth and in direct contact. It is at this point that Soul will reveal the answer.

Learn the value of contemplation just before retiring and upon awakening. It is to your advantage that at these points of change in consciousness awareness that we find a good time to contemplate. Therefore the problems won't be taken into your sleep state to cause them to penetrate deeper into the human consciousness and become fixed. On the other hand if you do your contemplation periods every morning, or that of the spiritual exercises, you will be able to start the day right by moving into the higher awareness.

There is the fixed idea in man that he is hardly anything more than flesh and blood which is impermanent in this world. He must learn to understand that he is Soul, above all this. This idea of impermanency is subjected and conditioned to limitation and being subjected to the environment. However every chela in ECK must break this idea, rise above it and step free of the idea of duality.

Every night before retiring, relax on the bed and watch the going to sleep process. Keep the attention at the point between the eyebrows. As the body relaxes and the mind settles down, and the change of viewpoint takes place which we call sleep, maintain the attitude of awareness from the upper levels. You will note that the body gets quiet, the thoughts settle down, the hearing is the last to leave the human consciousness. You will be detached on the borderline state, as though in a dream. Then you will come into the state of beingness which is characterized by the clarity of mental vision, not an unconscious state of a mental fog but a level of awareness beyond the limits of mortal expression.

This viewpoint may last a moment, or for several hours, and eventually it may last through the whole night. But while the body is resting you awaken in the Atma Sarup (Soul body) which is when we find ourselves in eternity, the overcoming of death. This is the freedom which is spoken so much about in ECKANKAR.

In this state one often sees the past lives which is good because this makes for a better understanding. But if you open the reservoir of the various bodies of yourself to look at past lives via hypnosis, it is to the average person a very disturbing experience. Many experienced or advanced persons in ECK can progress spiritually to that point of unfoldment where the past is revealed to them. But they are also at that point of understanding that they can dismiss it without a moment's notice, with the realization that it was much like the events of their present daily life and that all life lies in the present.

There are two kinds of people who cannot be hypnotized by the ordinary means. The first type is that person who has an aberration against being hypnotized because of fear. The second type is impossible because he has the realization that, in ECK, mind is a lower part of himself, and that he can control it regardless. Self-hypnotism is a part of this overall idea and should not be indulged in because of the problems which may arise from it.

People who try to condition themselves in the belief that they are of the higher consciousness, when they are not really in this state are simply deluding themselves. Often conditioning the mind by affirmations and meditations will not be of any advantage to the participant. A consciousness conditioned to the states of prosperity, emotional stability and health, is only working in the social areas of life. But this is of course the human way of doing things, using the creativeness of the mind and which of course will not last. Long as the chela is reacting whether it be in a positive or negative manner, if it's compulsively a reaction, he is bound to this world by secondary causes.

True contemplation releases men from conditioning so that he can see true reality, so that he is free from compulsive behavior and finds a true set of values.

Lots of people are intrigued with the possibility of making progress through sleep learning, by having a record or tape recording with some constructive message played during the twilight sleep hours. This can be done of course, and is not at all a bad idea. The period of the in-between sleep and awakening which is called the twilight sleep, just after one drops off to sleep is a good time for this because the analytical mind is closed off. It is the part of the mental apparatus which monitors the inflow of the senses and their experiences, and files it according to the conditioned reflexes. Then the unconscious, which accepts anything introduced to it is wide open.

Anyone can work with this through sleep learning. But it is best to de-condition the mind, rather than condition it to certain suggestions, to remove existing blocks and patterns, by doing away with aberrations which always come up from past lives. It will be possible to have such tapes from ECKANKAR ASOST, sometime.

Moving from the sleep state to another interesting subject is the study of the aura. The aura is a subtle, magnetic emanation generated by the etheric and other forces of the being or object with which it is connected.

Everything in nature generates its own aura, atmosphere or magnetism. This is quite true of the lowest crystal and of the living organism, of the lowest to the highest conscious entity known as man. The way to grasp this is to consider the common magnet. Around its poles there exists a sphere of influence known as the magnetic field through which pass lines of force between one pole and the other. The existence of this field is known by the

106

influence of the magnet upon light iron filings. When these are put at random on a sheet of paper they will respond to a magnet beneath without contact and will follow the magnet in its movements. The more sensitive the filings the greater is the distance at which their response can take place. Movement of an electrical circuit across these lines of magnetic forces converts the motion into power, and this power can be transformed into light, heat, or other forms of energy.

In the human organism there are forces like this, the forces of electricity and magnetism. Each person possesses a magnetic field which is the aura. It radiates from each individual, as solar rays emanate from the sun. The human aura receives the essential qualities of the etheric, the astral, causal, mental and the spiritual forces of the individual. In a vital sense, every human being creates his own magnetic atmosphere, which unfailingly reveals the temperament, disposition, character and the condition of health.

Its existence is evidenced in various ways. For example when charged with high potential electricity, the aura itself becomes electrified. This illumination occurs within a definite boundary which is variable around the body. It may be a matter of inches in one part and possibly a number of feet in another, while there may be rays projected in a straight line for a matter of five or six feet. It is possible to make a definite reading of the aura of the individual. All ECK Masters have been able to read auras whenever they wish but never reveal anything until requested.

The halo round the head of an ECK Master is no poetical fiction, no more than the invisible aura or sphere of life radiating from a precious stone. Sometimes this aura is not restricted to the head but is depicted as surrounding the whole body with a misty glow or luminous cloud. Moses' face gleamed when he came down from the mountain with the stone tablets which is a proof of power of his aura being alighted with the great spirit of ECK.

We also find that minerals as well as other things with life send out auras. Copper, carbon and arsenic will send out auras of red. Lead and sulphur emit blue auric colors. Gold, silver and antimony give off green, and iron gives off every color of the spectrum. Plants and animals emit similar colors according to their innate characteristics, while humans will express their own individual aura colors by what we know as color tones.

Those who have not attained the sight of clairvoyance can sense the presence of the aura by the conscious feeling of the strange power which some people who have strong, forceful personalities, carry with them. These people may not seem to be spiritual, or even intellectuals but the very force of their personality seems to radiate from them.

The aura is a kind of subtle extension of the character which is capable of both giving and receiving impressions, and through this medium we make conscious contact quite apart from the physical senses. One might feel the instinctive attraction or repulsion, as the case may be. We can give no reason however the attraction and repulsion speak of an intrinsic harmony or disharmony between the auras. This is why I have often spoken of psychic space which might crowd other individuals, or give them space for freedom of their own.

An explanation of the aura can be found in the nature of man which is made up of the three basic principles, the astral, causal and mental. These constitute a person's being which make up the aura in the human consciousness. There is of course the spiritual which, although it belongs to a different order of consciousness, also manifests through the aura.

The counterpart or the secondary body is that vehicle of the life-forces which flows into the physical body from the outer world, from the atmosphere, the sun, planets, cosmic rays. It vitalizes and sustains the physical body. Death is the translation of the functioning of this body called the lunar, or unconscious body on the physical plane. Interpenetrating the unconscious body which is the form from the subconscious or unconscious self, is the astral body, the vehicle of emotions, desires and passions. It is this body which usually has the brilliant everchanging radiations that the clairvoyants see when describing the aura.

The astral body is in turn interpenetrated by the causal body, which is the seed body for causes and effects. This is the area of the time track which gives the incarnations of Soul on the earth plane. It often deceives the clairvoyant who may think this is the final place for reading. This body is, in its turn, interpenetrated by a more refined and subtle structure, termed the mind, or mental body, the vehicle of thought visible to seers as a circle of light around the head. If it is the body of that which is called the Soul plane the nimbus is likely to be light of Soul.

These bodies, or zones overlap each other. The lunar or unconscious body, which is really a part of the mental body which runs the subconscious parts of the body, constitutes the inner aura, and extends only a little beyond the physical form. The astral body is egg shaped and forms the second aura, the causal body is a more round form, and the mental body forms a less defined structure in the outer aura. Soul forms about the head as stated before.

Of course there are more subtle emanations depending on the development of the individual's spiritual self. In some persons who are of a devout, unselfish nature, the spiritual aura which is of course that of Soul is very pronounced and beautiful, while in others of an animal-like nature there is not too much to view. Habitual thought will color the aura more than anything else.

The nature of the area of the aura's development and extension will depend upon the unfoldment of Soul and mind in the individual. These inner forces in primitive people will be rudimentary, while in intelligent and highly developed people they will be strong and forceful. There is the texture of aura to be considered also, which varies according to the individual, the brutal and refined, sensitive and insensitive, the choleric and placid, in different types of auras according to their disposition and character.

The aura is further rendered complex and diversified by the varied play of the emotions, passions and feelings. These impart a definite color tone to the auric radiation. The study of the colors and their meaning will be given in another chapter in this book.

The aura is also an unfailing guide to the health condition of the individual. In good health the vital rays or forces stream into the auric atmosphere imparting to it a clear, radiant brilliance; in failing health the color tones are dull and dark, while the disease is indicated by varied spots or patches over the areas affected.

There is talk about aura adjusting which seems to have gained some mention here. The aura cannot be adjusted by anyone no matter what is said for here we have a situation that concerns healing. The healing of any individual doesn't come in the aura or this area at all. It is within the spiritual body, which is the higher one, or one of the psychic bodies which have been named here and not the aura.

The human atmosphere is the invisible influence at work in all contacts, business, social, emotional and home. It explains why some people are a source of inspiration and personal power influencing all those who come within the sphere of their influence, those who are spoken of as having magnetic personalities, like preachers, doctors, politicians and others. Those who have a lesser degree of magnetism are the ordinary persons who are attracted and energized by the ones with the powerful auras, similar in manner to the small iron filings which are irresistibly drawn into the magnetic field of influence.

It is well known that the auras of the ordinary persons may become polarized by the influence of a powerful personality and they may in turn become lighted with a brightness which can be imparted to them. This is why so many people in India will stay around an ashram in hopes that some of the light of their master will rub off on them. It was well known that after Confucius died that many hundreds of his followers stayed about his tomb in hopes some of his intellectual enlightenment would rub off on them. The descendants of these originals were still there 600 years later still in hopes of finding some enlightenment.

The far reaching effects of the aura is well known to every one in ECKANKAR. Some persons with good harmony are the centers of health, love and happiness to all within their sphere. Their presence cheers and upbuilds those in sympathy with them, while it has a counteracting influence upon others less well disposed. Angular, vicious and unhappily developed persons cause others to be repelled. A strong positive aura reacts upon the weak, negative kind as a fully charged battery will disseminate its charge if connected with a weaker one. On the other hand a weak, depleted aura, indicating reduced vitality, acts as a psychic sponge or vampire on those around and saps their energy.

It is very interesting to note that there are certain cases where the Lunar body leaves the physical organism and withdraws the vitality, such as when a hand or leg goes to sleep. The Lunar counterpart may be seen by the ECK Master hanging outside the physical arm or leg until the vitality returns to the temporary dead limb. Sometimes in hypnosis the head of the Lunar body divides and hangs outside the physical head, one half over the shoulder, or around the neck like a collar. When anaesthetics are used the Lunar body is partially driven out and if the application is too strong and prolonged then death results.

The aura is the sum-total of thought forces and emotions, the Lunar, Astral, Mental and Soul of the individual. The interpretation of the aura is in the thoughts and feelings collected around the physical frame in the form of fine, vibratory waves or rays of color. Vibration is the key word to the aura, and the colors are really vibration possessing a symbology of their own. The colors expressed as follows are important in reading the aura: White – the true spiritual power. Yellow is the color of Soul power. Indigo is intuition. Blue is for wisdom. Green is for energy. Orange is for health and red is for life.

The ancient Egyptians were believed to be the first to formulate the doctrine of correspondence between colors and the human consciousness, but the ECK Masters knew about this many centuries before the Egyptians brought it to light for man to study. Each of the bodies of man, or his modes of consciousness, are related somewhat to the basic primary colors, red, blue and yellow which symbolize the physical body, the mental body and Soul body. From this trinity emanates or evolves the secondary colors which are: orange, green, indigo and the sub colors of grey and others. White and black are the opposite poles in the aura. White stands for true spirituality and black for evil. There are also gold, pink, silver and brown in the colors of the aura.

To break down the colors for analysis we find that Red is the symbol of life. Those people who have a great deal of red in their auras have strong physical characteristics, strong minds and wills and a materialistic outlook on life. Dark red is an indication of selfishness. Cloudy red indicates greed and cruelty. Bright reds reveal generosity and good ambitions. When red is the main color in the aura it shows leadership, the type called magnetic personality.

The orange color is that of health and vitality. Bright orange is good health, while dull reddish orange is selfishness and pride. Strong orange color indicates a vital, energetic, active personality. These type people are usually rulers but good ones who can manage others and take responsibility.

Yellow is a good aspect of Soul development. Bright yellow is for those who are capable in this world, and indicates courage and hope. Pale yellow indicates the higher development of Soul. Muddy yellow shows impractical natures of people who are visionaries.

Green in the aura is a good sign. This shows individualism, energy and regeneration. Dark green shows the negative aspects which are envy, jealousy, deceit and treachery.

Blue in the aura represents inspiration and divine wisdom. It is the color of fortune, self-reliance and confidence and positivity. It is a sign of sincerity and idealism. The pale shades of blue show integrity, divine wisdom and Soul development.

Grey in the aura means love of convention, formality, tendency toward narrow-mindedness. Heavy grey could mean meanness and dullness. These people are a prodding type who do all jobs with a thoroughness. It is the lone wolf type and the individual who likes to do it his own way.

Violet is the color of the subconscious mind. It has the elements of vitality and power. It has long been associated with power and influence especially in the western church and among the kings and potentates of ancient times. These people are noted for their ambitions to express their own will over masses of people.

Black is not a color but the negation of it. It has always been associated with dark deeds, the devilry and evilness. For the churchmen to wear black is an indication of their leaning toward a lack of vitality and misunderstanding of colors. In the East the priestcraft has not made this mistake and has worn yellows and blues. The most depraved Souls have auras which are seen to glow with a crimson red shot with black. This is the most vicious combination of evil colors known.

Pink in the aura denotes, a quiet, refined, modest type of person. This color seldom shows up in the aura of positive, dogmatic or aggressive people. It manifests frequently in people who like a quiet life and are fond of beauty and artistic surroundings. Those with pink in their aura will have long and lasting devotions to their mates and friends. The successful nun, in the church, usually has a strong mixture of pink and blue in her aura.

Those with silver in their aura are generally volatile and lively but very unreliable people. It is a color that goes with persons who are versatile, active, and gifted in all matters which pertain to movement, speech, travel and activism. These people are very often dabblers in all trades and professions, but masters of none. Where silver dominates be on your guard for there is feebleness, inconstancy and changing moods in the individual.

Brown is not a bad color in the aura as so many people expect. It denotes a capacity for organization and orderly management. It is the color for a business person and stands for industry. Do not expect strong emotional feelings or tendencies in brown tinged auras. It is the ruling color of conventions and the rigid type of minds. But it is the starting point for ambition and power, materialistic and commercial, and has given the individual a painstaking perseverance. When mixed with green it shows selfishness, the grabbing instinct. The lighter shades of brown show avarice in the individual. The muddy brown shows sickness especially over the areas where the ailment may be.

CHAPTER 8

THE STRANGE BOOKS OF THE ECK ADEPTS

The ancient order of ECK Adepts are those Masters of ECKANKAR whose main duty is the guardianship of the Shariyat-Ki-Sugmad, the sacred scriptures of this mysterious brotherhood. They are well hidden and seldom seen by the eyes of the profane, although it's known that they are now being translated from the invisible worlds into the humanistic languages.

These writings as mentioned many times are distributed in sections from this world through to the highest plane. A particular section of the Shariyat-Ki-Sugmad is in a Temple of Golden Wisdom, guarded by a particular ECK Master, on each plane. Each ECK Master, who is such a guardian is also the preceptor of these sacred writings which are under him.

When an ECK chela becomes adapted to Soul Travel, the Mahanta, the Living ECK Master, begins to take him nightly, during his dream state, to one of the Temples of Golden Wisdom where he begins his study of the ECKANKAR. He usually begins at the Katsupari Monastery, in the northern Tibetan mountains, going upward to other Temples of Golden Wisdom when he has successfully progressed, to where he is taken every night in his dream state by the living ECK Master.

These books have certain sections which give prophecies, give much wisdom on the ECK-Vidya and work out many problems of man. Therefore we begin to think about them in terms of value and mystery, giving out only that data which the human self can handle at his stage of spiritual progress. When he starts moving past the lower things of life, then the living ECK Master takes him higher into the divine wisdoms of ECKANKAR, the true aspect of life; that is, it is life itself.

The Shariyat-Ki-Sugmad is therefore a series of sacred writings which contains the deepest and most vital divine knowledge and Godly wisdom in any collection of writings anywhere within the universes of God. All others are pale beside these writings for they contain not only prophecies but the revelations of the SUGMAD (God) to the orthodox religions.

Those who seek the wisdom of the Shariyat-Ki-Sugmad cannot find it except through the spiritual assistance of the living ECK Master. It is he alone who is responsible for taking the individual into the other worlds to study with the varied ECK Masters who teach out of the books of the Shariyat-Ki-Sugmad. Here they learn those prophecies such as when the world is going to come to an end through the terrible destruction of fire and water; the drowning of the city of Los Angeles and most of the west coast by earthquakes and the sea; the terrible moon plague which will visit the earth and destroy much of its population; the upheaval of the central plains of eastern Europe and the formation of a new chain of mountains; the assassination of the various political figures of nations of the world, and the awful devastation of World War III.

These books also give the triumph of the yellow race and the red tyrant who will sit upon the necks of the masses of people. They speak of the Mahanta, the living ECK Master, who comes again to save the world from complete destruction, and to return as many Souls to the heavenly kingdom as possible during his reign on earth.

The prophecies of Nostradamus will be forgotten after one reads and studies those revelations which are in the ninth book of the Shariyat-Ki-Sugmad. They give many of the forthcoming things which will affect this world and the others beyond this physical realm.

The ancient Temples of Golden Wisdom are often the subject of much discussion by many who are seeking spiritual truths, and have either heard about them, or have been fortunate to have been taken to them in the Nuri Sarup, during the sleep state. Yet much of this talk is based upon hearsay and legends and myths have grown up around them. However any of those who have had the opportunity to visit any of these magnificent archives of the true wisdom will vouch for the authenticity of their existence.

There is a major existing Temple of Golden Wisdom on every one of the inner planes of God, including two on this planet, one on Venus, and one successively on those five spirito-material, and

116

seven spiritual planes, even into the heart of the SUGMAD. There is a segment or better known as a book of the Shariyat-Ki-Sugmad located in each of the Temples of Golden Wisdom, in each of these planes, and there is an ECK Master who is always the guardian of these individual sections of the book.

These are gathering places for those who travel consciously or unknowingly during sleep. They are usually taken by the living ECK Master to one of these fountains of knowledge to gather esoteric wisdom. But it is seldom if at any time that the individual concerned is ever taken to the Atma Lok (Soul plane) in the sleep state. When one goes to this plane under the escort of the living ECK Master he is fully conscious of what is taking place.

Many of the ECK Masters who have formerly lived and served their apprenticeship in the lower worlds have established themselves on the various planes in these ancient temples of wisdom, to teach those Souls who visit these places under the guidance of the ECK Masters. However, one should beware of those individuals who have designated themselves as Masters, and are not in the least anything which they claim. Mastership is that lofty position of a long line of Masters who have existed in the past, and have handed down the spiritual mantle to their chosen successor. These have been men, like you and I, who have reached perfection in their spiritual bodies and have been established as a line of spiritual rulers for years, often centuries. Those who claim mastership by appointment from any other source are false prophets. This is especially true in the field of ECKANKAR, for all its Masters come from a distinctive long line of spiritual hierarchy stretching back into the misty eons before time on this earth.

The Temples of Golden Wisdom are located in the various places and are under the guidance of the adepts so named: The Katsupari Monastery in northern Tibet, where the Temple of Golden Wisdom is under the guardianship of Fubbi Quantz, the famed ECK Master of the sacred scriptures of the Shariyat-Ki-Sugmad (Way of the Eternal) and first section of these ancient records.

The other school in this physical universe is at Agam Des, the spiritual city in the remote Himalayan mountains. Its name means inaccessible world. We must go in Soul form to listen and study the wisdoms there. This temple is called the Temple of Gare-Hira, under the great ECK Master, Yaubl Sacabi, the guardian of that part of the Shariyat-Ki-Sugmad which is the sacred scripture on

117

the altar of the inner sanctum. Agam Des is the home of the Eshwar-Khanewale (the God Eaters) for they partake of the cosmic spirit like we do material foods.

The next Temple of Golden Wisdom is the House of Moksha in the city of Retz on the planet Venus. Here we find the ECK Master, Rami Nuri in charge of that section of the Shariyat-Ki-Sugmad. He personally teaches those who visit the Moksha temple in their own dream state, with the living ECK Master. It is a beautiful building with a dome structure which is made of some type of material like glass through which the light flows in a gentle manner.

The ECK Master Rami Nuri stands in the center of the room, which is round, surrounded by those who have come to the House of Moksha to explain and demonstrate that section of the Shariyat-Ki-Sugmad. He is a rather tall man with dark features, has a very short beard which is white as is his hair. His eyes are dark and flashing.

The astral plane has their school of Golden Wisdom in the temple of Askleposis, in the city of Sahasra-Dal-Kanwal. It is under the guidance of Gopal Das, the ECK Master, who has made a great name for himself, on both the earth and astral planes. He is a rather tall, thin man with light golden hair and a full face, with light blue eyes.

The temple of Askleposis is a rather odd building, constructed along the lines of the temples in India. It sits rather high off the ground with huge columns, made of stone as well as the rest of the building, with broad steps leading up to the entrance. The building is made of some sort of rose stone which gleams in the light of the astral day.

Gopal Das teaches from a small dais to those who visit there under the direction of the living ECK Master. His audience sits on the floor before him looking directly at him and never upward. It is the policy of the ECK Masters never to appear to be above others, even in the matter of heights.

The next school of wisdom is in the temple of Sakapori, the causal plane of the other worlds. It is piloted by that great ECK Master known as Shamus-i-Tabriz, a Sufi, who lived several hundred years ago on this physical plane. He was the Master of Jalal-din-Rumi, thirteenth century Persian poet and sage, a follower of ECK and a Master.

Shamus-i-Tabriz is of medium height, wears a short, brown beard, a white turban, and has dark, flashing eyes. He is a true master of ECK wisdom, and those who are able to travel this far have certainly been fortunate. He is an able instructor in the Shariyat-Ki-Sugmad and the few who come here leave well versed in this section of the sacred scriptures.

The mental plane has the famed ancient Temple of Golden Wisdom in the city of Mer Kailash. It appears very much like the ancient temple of Diana which was at the city of Antioch during the early Christian era when St. Paul visited that city and preached against the Greek religions. The science of ECKANKAR was once taught in this temple of Diana.

The ECK Master in charge of this section of the Shariyat-Ki-Sugmad, is Towart Managi, an African holy man during the ancient days in that country which is known as Abyssinia, formed out of the four olden kingdoms. He is rather small, looks frail and delicate, has close cropped white hair and a small white beard. He speaks from a low dais on which he sits in the lotus fashion.

The next Temple of Golden Wisdom is located in the Etheric world in the city of Arhirit. This is the city of light, with its flaming pale blue flames sweeping upward in the sky; it would make anyone approaching it be in awe because of its terrible beauty. The temple is gigantic, much larger than anything that could be found in any of the lower worlds. It appears to be made in gothic structure with two huge towers, like wings reaching far into the sky. It is a greyish sandstone building which glitters in the sunlight like a million diamonds. It is similar to that which John, the Christian apostle spoke about in the Book of Revelations. It makes one wonder if it was this temple and city of Arhirit which he witnessed during his mystical state.

Lai Tsi, a high Chinese spiritual Master, who is an adept in the Ancient Order of Vairagi, is the faultless guardian of the sacred scriptures placed in this Temple of Golden Wisdom in the city of Arhirit. This temple is named the temple of Karakota, and is in the center of the city.

Lai Tsi is almost tiny in stature, being about five feet and a half in height, wears a flat Chinese hat, has a small white goatee and thin, wrinkled face with sunken dark eyes. He wears an embroidered robe which is dark maroon in color. He speaks with a slow manner that seems hard to hear, but those who listen always understand perfectly what he has to say.

The next school of the Temples of Golden Wisdom is that of the temple of Param Akshar, the house of the imperishable knowledge. This is on the fifth plane, which is called the Atma Lok, the Soul plane. This is the dividing line between the universal mind worlds, the lower regions and the true spiritual worlds of the SUGMAD.

The temple is located in the city of Akshar, which is a glorious place of the higher worlds. There is a community of ECK Masters near this temple, for the headquarters of the Vairagi Adepts is located within the temple. But the guardian for this section of the Shariyat-Ki-Sugmad is that renowned ECK Master Tindor Saki, who has been instrumental in bringing about so many changes in the policies of ECK being brought into the open in the world today, so that all peoples will be exposed to it and can take up its path as desired.

Tomo Geshig is a thin, lanky being, not so much in form as being a halo in light. Those who enter into the true spiritual worlds do not do so in what we consider the human form, but as a light, which this ECK Master appears to be in at the time of viewing him. But this is the second of the true worlds of spirit and the feeling here is that one who visits them is in a dream state, for everything is wavering and in such appearance that we do not seem to find anything to be taken for granted.

The Temple of Golden Wisdom on the seventh plane is really not a temple or structure as would be recognized on the lower planes. However, the Shariyat-Ki-Sugmad here is under the guardianship of Mesi Gokaritz, who was one of the great ECK Masters in the early days of Greece. This is the Alaya Lok plane and its sound is Hum which is a humming sound and can carry very high vibrations with it. Everything here is in the great cosmic white light and the great cosmic sound. The two are so combined that one cannot tell the difference, and the form again is a lighter aura of white light.

All in this world, as those which have started from the beginning of the Atma, the Fifth plane which is known as the Soul plane, everything including the study of the Shariyat-Ki-Sugmad has been for divine knowledge. Within the spirito-material worlds, or the psychic planes everything has been divine information.

We find here three divisions of knowledge which one receives when studying the Shariyat-Ki-Sugmad, first is divine information which is found in those worlds such as the physical, astral, causal, mental and etheric planes. Divine knowledge is gained on the four planes of the worlds of the spiritual loks. These are: The Atma Lok, the Alakh Lok, the Hukikat Lok, and the Agam Lok.

Third, the divine wisdom comes from the Agam Lok, the Anami Lok and the SUGMAD Lok which is the final plane of all, and often called the Ocean of Love and Mercy.

Therefore you see that not many people will have complete wisdom while serving in the physical body because few besides the ECK Masters ever reach into these heavenly worlds.

However, we find that the next world in which the Shariyat-Ki-Sugmad is located is the eighth plane, called the Hukikat Lok. Lok always means plane. The sacred writings are within a structure known as the temple of the Aluk, which is also the sound word of that plane. It is surrounded by a very brilliant light and the ECK Master who is in charge here is Kadmon, one of the highest of the ECK adepts in the Order of the Vairagi. He was on earth during the very early times when man was in his infancy.

Within this book of the Shariyat-Ki-Sugmad are the strange prophecies of ECKANKAR which give the end of the world in the lower regions, and many of the disasters which will fall upon the human race, as well as those for the other planets within this system. It will give the beginning of the new golden age in this world, and follow through on the prophecies of the various ages which are to follow. Some of these prophecies are amazing and will not be repeated here, but it means that the end of this dark age, the Kali Yuga is coming about in a few thousand years. It will go out in fire and destruction. It also tells about the tremendous earthquake which is coming on the west coast which will wipe out miles of land, cause destruction of property and the loss of many lives.

About one hundred and fifty years later, following this disaster there will come the vast upheavals of the present land masses caused by violent volcanic actions. These will not only destroy what is known as the United States, but most nations and countries of the world. The complete map of the earth land masses will be changed as new continents rise out of the seas to reform the world again.

Only these new continents will not be new at all, for they are the ancient lands known as Mu and Atlantis, which are prominent in legend and myth but were reality in ancient history.

In the meantime the world will be struck with the moon plague which will take off millions of people. Other disasters will strike until the whole human race will turn again to the Supreme Diety, the SUGMAD, asking for help against all the plagues of the world.

There is the prophecy of World War III, which will bring about a vast destruction of humanity. There is also the prophecy about the red dictator who will come out of the east to try and conquer the world again like Khubla Khan, but after terrible battles and destructions of cities and people he will be conquered in his intention to be the world leader by the sword. Thereafter will be petty wars and small tyrants who are trying to establish themselves. But each fails as they attempt to set up kingdoms of their own.

There will also be a migration of the human race to other planets, some of which will be found to be similar to the earth world in their climate and vegetation. Some of the planets will be found to be inhabited by certain types of humanoids. These are the ones who man the space crafts and in time there will be a mighty war between planets. These wars will devastate the planets and leave room for those who will try to leave the earth planet, and settle on others.

Leaving this plane we enter into the Agam Lok, which is the first of the divine wisdom planes. Here the Shariyat-Ki-Sugmad is again light and sound, however the sound is greater than any of its other elements. It is here that one learns the music of woodwinds which has that aspect of divine wisdom for whoever should reach this plane, few as they are. And those who do are great in their information, knowledge and wisdom of the divine. All else is pale in comparison with what they know.

The ECK Master who is in charge of the Shariyat-Ki-Sugmad here is a being we can call Agnotti. Just who he is nobody seems to know, however there was an ECK Master by this name during the earliest times on earth, when man was in his most primitive stages of development. The Shariyat-Ki-Sugmad is kept in a place called the temple of Akash, near a community of ECK Masters, who live together as part of the Ancient Order of the Vairagi. But there is no way to tell what Agnotti's appearance might be because he appears in different forms to different Souls.

It is here that Soul enters into that heavenly state and first experiences what is known as God-Realization. The heights of the Agam Lok (plane) is what makes it difficult to reach in spiritual travel and Soul development. Persistence and patience brings about success if one wants to reach this world.

The next plane is the Anami Lok, or the nameless world. It is here that one gets lost in the sound and light unless he has the guidance and protection of the Mahanta, the living ECK Master. This is the world where the sounds are that of a gigantic whirlpool, sucking and spewing out the dregs which enter into it. It is here that the higher degree of God-Realization is gained and the divine wisdom begins to pour into each Soul which visits this world.

It is within this plane that each Soul which visits here enters into that phase of contemplation which is known as the Nirvikalpa. It is a form of deep contemplation in which the contemplator cannot distinguish himself from the object of his attention, which is the Shariyat-Ki-Sugmad.

From here he passes into the highest plane known as the true heavenly home, that in which the SUGMAD dwells, the first cause of all things. Here it's found that the Shariyat-Ki-Sugmad is not actually a book of writings, but the very wisdom pouring out of the heart of the Supreme Deity. It is consistent and wondrous. There are no words to speak of it and therefore no one can put into vocalization anything nor write anything which is found in this world.

These are the strange books of the ECK Adepts. So far very little has been written on them, but in the course of time most of them will be translated out of the invisible worlds and brought forth into the worlds of the visible so that man can be enlightened and uplifted. They are given here in this book simply to let the world know they exist and that many times when anyone is giving an ECK-Vidya reading that these readings might be intermingled with the Shariyat-Ki-Sugmad, for so many times the life of every Soul is dictated by these strange books; and that many times the readings might be found in Soul records almost identical with the works of ECK, for ECK Itself is life.

All that is in the nature of man and Soul is found in the Shariyat-Ki-Sugmad. The dream method of teaching is one way by which those looking for truth and the future, can visit the various temples in the presence of the Mahanta, the living ECK Master. The ECK Master will take him out of his physical body nightly, to visit the appropriate plane whenever the chela is suited for his spiritual advancement. The ECK Masters named here in charge of the various Temples of Golden Wisdom are Masters in the field of

123

the ECKANKAR line of mastership. Each is capable of the true initiation which is the spiritual duty of any ECK Master.

These ECK Masters were once inexperienced Souls like anyone now living in the physical body, but in the course of their spiritual evolution finally reached the heights of the Divine Reality, and became a true Satguru, and a co-worker with the SUGMAD. This should give hope to all who enter into the path of ECK.

The Naacal records which are said to be the first of the sacred writings known contain scattered references to ECKANKAR. Those two monasteries in the mountains of Tibet and along the eastern slopes of the Hindu Kush mountains, in Agam Des, which have the first two sections of the Shariyat-Ki-Sugmad are extremely well hidden. They are so well kept out of the sight of anyone in search for them that it's doubtful that many can find them, not even the Buddhist lamas who have gained the power of moving about the ether at their own volition. The keepers of these records are careful in their guardianship of them for nobody can enter these monasteries unless first screened by a group of ECK monks who can read the seeker's aura as we can scan a daily newspaper.

ECKANKAR is closer to being in Its original form than any of the philosophical or religious teachings today. It is neither a religion, philosophy, nor metaphysics, for it is the path to the SUGMAD that we call the ECK-Marg, meaning of course, the path of ECKANKAR.

The Shariyat-Ki-Sugmad consists of twelve sections, each about thirty thousand words made up of cantos or verses, or simply written forms, and sometimes in dialogue. It is said to be the words of the SUGMAD speaking to ITS chela Sat Nam, the first embodiment of ITSELF in the lower worlds.

The opponents of the ECK-Vidya frequently advance the argument that belief in the influence of the records and the Shariyat-Ki-Sugmad leads to a fatalistic attitude toward all problems of life. We like to think of ourselves as free agents in all the works of life, but it's found that there is restraint both psychological and physical, at which we chafe constantly. We like to talk about free countries, free speech and free trade, and the very thought of freedom becomes a fetish. We rise up in righteous wrath against anyone seeking to curb the spontaneous abandon of our actions.

Therefore we acknowledge no authority superior to our own

desires, which is actually the Kal at work. The democratic form of government is supposed to have released us from supervision and restraint, but the equality complex seems to overcome most of us.

It is here that the ECK-Vidya steps in with the knowledge that each of us makes our karma. The vast pageantry of cosmic order manifests throughout its every part of the worlds of the SUGMAD in an absolute and immutable law. But the very thought of this law of the universe oppresses and disturbs the lawless mortals of any generation of men. Man hates to think that he is a mere atom moved by inevitable and immutable laws, and this is what disturbs him in an ECK-Vidya reading. His ego which is the most easy part of him to be offended becomes hurt, and he is mortally injured by the immensities of what the ECK-Vidya reading has to say. It is for this very reason that he hardly wants to think of anything as immense as the sacred books of the Shariyat-Ki-Sugmad. He does not feel that anything so huge could be beyond the understanding of his senses, therefore he refuses to believe that the Shariyat-Ki-Sugmad exists.

It was among the wisest of nations in ancient times that ECK was accepted by many, in freedom not of worship but as a way of life. Nor was antiquity enfeebled by a sense of fatalism, rather it found itself in the recognition of immutable institutions of law in which no elements of change or accident existed. Having discovered and accepted the great laws of life, the philosophers of antiquity put their own lives in order, gladly acknowledging the sovereign wisdom which regulated justly and certainly all celestial and terrestrial affairs of the nations concerned.

The law of cause and effect which is the law of karma, working deeply within the individual, is one of the most important of the twelve great laws by which, according to the ancient wisdom, the universes are sustained. The acceptance of this law and the understanding of its inferences is found within the works of the Shariyat-Ki-Sugmad. This is the works which every ECK-Vidya reader uses someplace in his readings for others.

Whether or not we believe it this law is the basis for every person and nation which has ever existed in this universe. Unrecognized by most, this same law preserves all the consistencies of life and action. As the farmer plants the seed at a certain time of the year with the perfect assurance that it will grow, we should know that by planting a deed or action in this world it certainly will return to us, unless it's done in the name of the living ECK Master.

However, very few people apply the law of cause and effect to personal action, sometimes because of ignorance, but more often, as already observed, because the training of the modern man has caused him to feel that he is in some way superior to or apart from the ordinary edicts of nature.

The great Rebazar Tarzs once said, "Effect follows cause as the wheel of the cart follows the hooves of the ox." Since we live in a world completely ruled by a law of universal compensation, then we must abide by the ECK-Vidya reading because it is concerned mainly with the Karmic patterns of the individual on every one of the lower planes, the physical, astral, causal, mental and subconscious. Most of the miseries which now afflict suffering mankind are due to our ignoring the principle of karma in action. We do not sense the profound moral inference behind the story of sowing and reaping. Few if any will ever ask what repercussions good or bad will have upon his future or realize that his present is the result of what his past has been.

Astrology has little to do with man's life as he thinks, but the ECK has everything to do with the administration of karma. Life is eternally building, constantly improving vehicles, or bodies, for its own needs. Hence we turn to the thought of the much needed subject reincarnation, which modern religions have very little use for because of a lack of mention in their own sacred scriptures. However, it is the foundation of ECKANKAR, and found mentioned time and again in the Shariyat-Ki-Sugmad.

The proper study of life is life itself, as Yaubl Sacabi once wisely stated, "The only way to know thyself is to study thyself."

Reincarnation applied to man teaches that each Soul has already lived many thousands of times upon this earth in a different body, each body fitting Its needs for the times in which It existed in the flesh. Each life It has lived and the body that It assumed depended upon the law of Karma working in his particular case. The causes leading up to one's present existence are not always evident in this life, nor are the consequences, which arising from present actions, will manifest in some future life. The ancient ECK Masters believed that from the ECK-Vidya reading it was possible to discover certain specifics of the previous lives of man so that it could help him in his search for peace and happiness.

126

The law of cause and effect when applied particularly to human concerns, was called karma by the ancients. But the word does not mean fatalism, only compensation. When a man buys on credit, he creates a debt and must pay for that debt according to the law. In a material, economic transaction this would not be regarded as fatalism, but as a responsibility. Every action which a human being performs may be regarded as a cause, and every cause set in motion must have an effect consistent with itself. This is not fatality, this is compensation or karma.

In this age of the Kali Yuga it appears that we all like to hope that by some mysterious formula we can escape the responsibilities of destructive action. Most of us want to be selfish but we do not want to suffer the reactions of selfishness. We constantly break natural law, and we are all seeking some panacea which will remove from us the unhappy consequences of our indiscretions. This is why so many visit the church daily praying for their requests to be fulfilled. They hope to escape their indiscretions by the interference of their own God who will set aside the law because of their prayers.

We find that the theological doctrine of the forgiveness of sin is a salve to take away the sting from the reactions of iniquity, but the law of Karma can never be evaded regardless of how much anyone prays to get around it. All the evils that we do will return to us, as well as all the good, and there is no escape from any part of the law of Karma.

The law of compensation, or karma, has two distinct aspects. Good karma is the beneficent reaction of constructive action or deeds. Good causations produce like consequences, bring joy and security and the good things of life. Bad karma is the reaction of destructive action or deeds. Evil causes set in motion produce evil consequences, resulting in the miseries and misfortunes which afflict this present life.

When a man is born into this world, there are three factors working together, molding and modifying his existence here. The first is good karma, which brings certain privileges of happiness and improvement, and surrounds him with such good things as have been earned. The second is bad karma, which manifests as the difficulties of the hour and the apparent evil fatality which dogs his footsteps. The third factor is action itself, his individual expression which is constantly making new karma, good or bad, according to the merit of the action itself.

The works of ECK teach the individual to be modest in success which is good karma, patient in adversity which is bad karma, and constructive in all actions and deeds. A life so lived promises future lives of greater enlightenment and happiness. Thus we find that the law of Karma controls, among other things, the actual phenomenon of birth itself. The individual is born at the time which he has merited, and into opportunities suitable for the next stage of his development. Each person is in the place which he has earned for himself, and, if he is unhappy with his present conditions, then he must set up within himself the causes which will result in a better state.

The ECK is the mechanism which administers the law of Karma. The universe is vibrations and the interaction of the aspects of all life forces are constantly setting up fields of specialized vibrations. The incarnating entity of man is also a rate of vibration, modified by the karmic factors within himself. The incarnation of the individual is determined by these vibratory factors. He is born into circumstances consistent with the karmic modifications of his own nature. He is born when the ECK has arranged the patterns consistent with his own karma. With his first breath, man breathes in the world today and what he has merited comes to him through the ECK power and becomes the individuality determinant for his own life.

The ECK therefore is not merely sending some vibrations upon a poor, helpless mortal. It is really administrating universal justice, bestowing upon each according to his own works. This could not possibly be fatalism, it is compensation. One of the things which every chela in ECK must learn is to pay gladly the debts which he has incurred in life. All karma both good and bad, leads finally to enlightenment through experience.

It is very often possible to determine, to some degree, the karmic elements in life from the ECK-Vidya reading, for in many respects the nativity is a statement of indebtedness, a bill rendered to each of us when we are born. In it are set forth the debts and credits of karma as these apply directly to the present life. The path of progress is that which arises from the past actions and deeds, and it is most apt to be revealed to the ECK-Vidya reader when he looks at the qualities of the elements of karma in the requestor's past lives.

Therefore to be sane one must learn to be able to control his life and to control his life he must control matter. An insane person is one who is the victim of circumstances or material creation. If you cannot control your world, you are being controlled by it. As you control it, you are free; as it controls you, you are bound and limited, and eventually become afraid of it. You cannot control matter if you are a realist and believe in the solidness and eternal nature of it. You control matter when you see that it is but an extension of consciousness, and learn to break the crust of solidness. As you learn to manipulate it you learn to see through it and become free. Those who retreat from life and do nothing are just as bound in matter as those who are stuck in the concept of a solid universe.

Those who know anything about the ECK-Vidya soon learn that control is the greatest factor which they have to contend with for then they can manage their lives both past and future, and can then be able to read the books of the Shariyat-Ki-Sugmad in each of the Temples of Golden Wisdom regardless of whatever plane they exist upon.

CHAPTER 9

THE SACRED NUMBERS OF THE ECK-VIDYA

Words are symbols of ideas, but numbers are symbols of divine realities. Spiritual verities eternal in the heavenly worlds, are expressed of themselves periodically in the worlds of objectivity by certain numbers which are sacred in ECKANKAR.

Yaubl Sacabi, the great ECK Master, who is the head of the spiritual city of Agam Des, stated "The world is built upon the power of the ECK numbers, therefore numbers must be the key to the understanding of the world." Numbers then are a key to the ancient views on life, in its broad sense, including man and beings, and the evolution of the human race, spiritually as well as physically.

It is commonly believed that our present numerical system was invented by the early Jewish race, and later developed by the Arabs but this isn't true. As a matter of fact the ECK Masters were using a numerical system since the beginning of time on earth.

The Arabs' history of a numerical system said it was borrowed from the Hindus, for the Indian sages declare that it was revealed to them from devas, the angelic forces of their own religious hierarchy. The Pythagoreans, the followers of the great Greek philosopher who was an ECK Master in his times, asserted that the doctrine of numbers, the chief of all in esotericism, had been revealed to man by the celestial deities; that the world had been called forth out of chaos by sound or harmony, and according to the principles of musical proportion. These are but confirmations of the occult teachings that the science of numbers was not slowly evolved by primitive man learning to count on his fingers, which is deduced as the probable origin by esoteric investigators, but was a fully elaborated system of computation revealed to the responsible heads of various mystery schools and religions during the ancient

131

times by the Eck Masters of the Order of the Vairagi.

The sacred numbers of ECKANKAR were the symbols which were the origin of measures, that shadowed the creative law or design of things in the lower worlds. Reflection becomes more involved when it is considered that the power of expression of the law, exactly, by numbers clearly defining a system, was not the accident of the language, but its very essence, and of its primary organic construction. Therefore neither the language nor the mathematical system attached to it, could be of man's invention, unless both were founded upon a prior language which afterwards became obsolete.

It is well known that the Egyptians had a system of astronomical calculations some 50,000 years before Alexander the Great, which set off dates, months and years by mathematical numbers. This was the duo-decimal system, or method of reckoning by 12 in common use. It is by the use of this system in the construction of the pyramids, that the origin of the English foot of 12 inches has been traced. Among the early races the decimal system or reckoning by 10, was esoteric and known only to the higher initiates.

Much of the system which was in early use during these times was due to the efforts of Gopal Das who was the living ECK Master during these times. He introduced a simple system which was considered the duo-decimal system which is the reckoning by 12 in common use. The priestcraft tried to withhold it from the public, but he was able to give out enough information especially among the ECK disciples of his times, and gradually in the centuries that followed it became better known and eventually found favor in public education.

Naturally in the early days of man the decimal system was held sacred because the esoteric leaders thought it was received from the higher powers.

We know the decimal system was used by mankind of the earliest archaic ages, since the whole astronomical and geometrical portion of the secret sacerdotal language was built upon the number 10, or the combination of the male and female principles. The 10, being the sacred number of the universe, was secret and esoteric, both as regards the unit and cipher, or zero, the circle.

This is natural for the ECK Masters have always tried to enlighten the people and uplift them in every respect. They knew the dire results of the misuse, the perversion, debasement or reversal of any symbol, that which would save mankind from all the degradation and suffering which resulted from the fraudulent manipulation of these sacred symbols by man to acquire personal advance or power at the expense of his fellow man. For example, the acquiring of individual wealth at the expense of the community and mankind in general, such as the worship of the Beast, in contradiction to the creation of wealth through normal means, such as agriculture, mining and manufacturing.

The law of numbers does not belong to the realm of chance. Numbers are potent factors in the working out of divine law, hence no system devised by man for his own aggrandizement or advantage at the expense of others can ever succeed. It may seem so up to a certain point or until the cycle of that particular combination of numbers reverts back to its true rate of vibration or the key-note which belongs to that particular expression of the divine law, and fulfills its real mission.

From the days of creation to the Apocalypse.in the Bible, the great stress is made upon 3, 4, 7, and 12. In the Hindu scriptures, the Vedas and Upanishads, numbers underlie every hymn, and stress is made upon 1, 3 and 7. It is the same system upon which Vach, or the speech of Zoroaster was built.

It is impossible to become an adept and fully grasp the deep problems of the religious writings such as the Buddhists, Christian, Brahmanical or Zoroastrian books without a knowledge of the significance of numbers. The power of the mantram or hymn, or a reading from one of the religious books, varies with the numbers and syllables of the words, the rhythm of the meter and the vibrations of the tones used, in addition to the meaning of the words themselves.

The vibratory chants of the ECK sounds are based upon the numbers of 3, 9, 12, and sometimes 60. The latter 60 vibrations is the highest one can go, and it's seldom that anyone in the human body can get himself up this high; if he does it means that the body can be burned into a crisp. If one can learn to use words or symbols which signify the number 60 it's possible that he can have a long life, beyond the human space alloted to man today.

These numbers are assigned in the vibratory rate of those who are initiates in ECKANKAR, generally working from zero to 3, maybe 6, then 9 and finally up to 12. This is one reason why the individual cannot demand initiation in ECK and believe that he can get it. If he is ready for initiation then he will be notified some way by the Mahanta, the living ECK Master.

The Mantram or secret word which is given the chela at his initiation whether it be from the first to the twelfth depends upon what the Mahanta, the living ECK Master believes is possible for him to take without greatly upsetting him or harming him in any way. This is what makes the initiation in ECKANKAR the highest of all initiations. The intoning slowly of the secret word for each chela and with a rhythmic cadence produces a certain effect. If done quickly and sharply a different effect is produced. These effects are based upon the laws of vibrations and not upon the imagination, nor merely the results of suggestions. The nerves are like the strings of a musical instrument and try to respond and adjust themselves to the vibrations which have been set up. The effects are apparently different; some will strike the mind and emotions, the various bodies of man, and spiritual self, generally lifting the individual to higher vibrations and thus higher planes.

All manifestations of life, as they come into the outer world from the inner, flow along certain geometrical lines and follow laws of the same nature. Flowers, trees, metals and even the species of animals and men follow out certain forms in growth and development. Flowers and plants have an expression established by the number 2 which designates grace and beauty. In closer examination we find that each species of life is expressed in some geometrical relationship to the ECK, and each is the intimate expression of its own Soul relations of things.

This is also true of each individual in the human race. While there is a general number of 3 which represents the vibrations of every man personally, not all are up to this point in life. Some are beyond this and some below it in their states of consciousness, so it's up to the Mahanta, the living ECK Master, to pull each up to this rate of vibrations when he is initiated into ECKANKAR.

Each vibration, or expression, has its number, rate of vibrations, or wave length, its sound, color and form and its own place in the grand plan of the SUGMAD. We have the square, zero, triangle and the dot as the basic characteristic design of life. Soul of Itself has that geometrical pattern of zero, and its vibrations can be at the beginning of the vibratory rates, or at the ending. The beginning and ending simply means the start of Soul in this world and Its ending in this world. It goes no further than this in its vibratory rates long as it is not on the path of ECK. It is the symbol of the unmanifested Deity, the darkness of chaos from which light, sound and order appears.

The circle represents boundless space and limitless time in eternity. It marks off the space in which creation takes place, or the circle formed by the down pouring of the ECK, in both light and sound. It is much like the circle of light projected by a lamp, within which a picture appears. In other words it is the circle of the unmanifested zodiac circle, and that which the ECK Master uses for the ECK-Vidya reading.

The zero is called naught or no-thing because no thing has been manifested. It is the silence of non-being. It can be said to be the secret place of the ever invisible being, the Mahanta, the living ECK Master. We find that the Mahanta, the Master within man, is simply asleep and spiritual darkness is filling the inner space of the individual. When the personality sees no way of escape from the inner strife and storms it cries out in desperation "Please Mahanta, save me before I perish." Then the breath of life stills the storms within, the Mahanta appears inwardly to that individual and commands the conflicts and strifes to cease.

It is then that we move to the number 3 which is much a sacred symbol in ECKANKAR. The ECK Masters of the Ancient Order of the Vairagi knew and taught that the SUGMAD is one, because IT is infinite, and IT is triple because IT is ever manifesting. The number represents the manifestation of the SUGMAD in this world in the form of the Mahanta, the ECK, and the living ECK Master. This is the first manifesting stage however, it will be seen later that he appears in the six bodies.

The triangle is the symbol of divine love, also man, woman and the magnetic attraction between them united in the divine. It is divine love which overshadows and manifests through man and woman. For every true marriage in which human love reaches up and blends with divine love is a witness that it (divine love) has penetrated into and manifested through humanity. Therefore 3 is the number of the perfect marriage, or the masculine and feminine expression of human love united above the earth world in divine love, the completion of the triangle.

The triangle or number 3 is a symbol also of satisfaction. For the only true satisfaction is the response we feel to the ECK force pouring through some form of union with the divine. The only real satisfaction is experienced in the thrill of oneness which comes when the divine in each of us finds expression in manifestation on any plane, physical, mental or spiritual, from the thrill of some deed done in the name of the ECK Master.

As man and woman are the lords of creation so they must in turn become the redeemers of the lower kingdoms, by becoming a channel for the ECK power, and lift up all lower aspects of creation into a higher expression. It is as the Mahanta, the living ECK Master, says, "All that come to me shall be lifted up." As man and woman are united and lifted up the ECK within each draw all the lower opposites, in the lower planes, to themselves.

The misconception of living here as mates who do not seem in harmony is believing that they are not properly mated. The problem here is that as a married couple travels the path of God together, they are more apt in their spirtual unfoldment to grow further apart on the spiritual planes, and this leads to separation of thought, feeling and harmony on the physical plane, yet they do not separate in marriage.

Therefore, there may develop great inharmony on the physical plane, not because they are becoming less spiritual, but because they are unfolding and being drawn into different currents of force which do not harmonize. As the spiritual love of ECK ever seeks greater and more perfect expressions of harmony, whenever whatever physical harmony there may be at first has expressed itself, the ECK tends to separate them temporarily, that each may be able to manifest a higher state of spiritual growth. In such cases separation on the physical plane, instead of being a calamity, is a blessing and an absolute necessity for the spiritual advance of each.

Each mate should be very patient for they will come back again on the physical plane in a greater harmony and love than ever before. However, in the marital relations of the present times we find that these spiritual lines of force are woefully mixed and tangled, both through the karma of similar mistakes in the past and through allowing other considerations than divine love to bring about union on the physical plane.

The number 3 is the word made flesh and dwelling among us, for it is the base line or the magnetic attraction which unites the positive and negative forces and completes the triangle. When the individual has moved into the higher realms he finds that all life is a manifestation of the trinity or number 3, but since the ordinary man has not yet mastered its 3 expressions he is subject to them.

136

When he does he becomes the master of those forces around him.

Those who have become involved with the number 3 soon learn that to pronounce a word is to evoke a thought and make it present. That the magnetic potency of human speech is the commencement of every manifestation in the spiritual worlds. To utter a name is not only to define a being, or entity, but to place it under and establish it through the emission of the word to the influence of one or the ECK power. The word of speech of man is, quite unconsciously to himself, a blessing or a curse. They are in a certain sense, either venomous or health giving, according to the hidden influence attached by the supreme wisdom to their elements, that is to say, to the letters which compose them and the numbers correlative to these letters.

It is fitting that this speech or word should be a commandment of number 3 since 3 is a symbol of the trinity or the 3-fold expression of the law of good manifesting in all things.

The number 6 is primarily the number of the ECK force in the psychic worlds, the force back of evolution. It is the number of unrest and incompleteness in that it resents the unrest of the psychic forces which are incomplete and ever changing, striving for perfection. It is the number which represents the six bodies of the Mahanta, who dwells on every plane in the shape which he is known in the physical form. These planes are: physical, astral, causal, mental, etheric and Soul.

He is complete within his bodies and the knowledge of the worlds, but everything outside of him is not, hence the characteristics of the sixth number. This number therefore shows that the cause of all evolution is the urge to perfection inherent in every living thing. It is also the ladder of God, the Antaskarana along which the devas, the angelic forces, are continually descending and ascending.

The number 6 is also in man as the Buddhi, or Soul principle which cannot rest until It finds Its spiritual home and reaches perfection in the number 12. It is concerned with the secret which Soul must wrestle from the lower worlds which gives It the ever-working, rejuvenating and active power of the works of ECK. Unless Soul can work in the area of the 6th number It is really not making spiritual progress. Any reader of the ECK-Vidya can tell him if his vibratory rates are within this category.

Also this is the six pointed star, that which appears in the spiritual eye when one crosses over from the psychic worlds into the Atma Lok, which is actually the sixth plane, or again the first of the true spiritual planes. This star is the blue star that I have spoken so much about in the written works of ECKANKAR. This is the symbol of the eternal light and sound, and whoever can dwell in it finds themselves free of all vices and disease. In other words good health and those things which come with the higher life first appear at this point, where number 6 is prominent.

The 6th commandment which is "Thou shalt not kill," derives its esoteric significance from the meaning of the number 6. The ECK power forcing its way through the limitations of matter into more and more perfect manifestations will soon bring about the perfection of Soul. Since this ECK power animates all forms of life and is immortal, the only thing we can kill is the form of manifestation of the divine Deity, whether it be in humanity or in the lower kingdoms. The only sense in which man can kill is to separate any form of life from the ECK stream of life force, or to dam it up or to refuse to permit it to manifest. Therefore anything that we may do to retard the manifestation of the ECK force in humanity or the world is suppressing it, which is not likely, provided the ECK desires to make its presence manifest in some way. But the thing which we are really suppressing, or in a sense killing, is our own manifestation, which is our own spiritual evolution. Any ECK-Vidya reader can tell the readee what he is doing to harm himself by reading off his vibratory rates.

Every Soul is evolving toward the ultimate goal, but each passes through many deaths in many conditions, yet by the power of the ECK, and with the ECK, he must ultimately triumph over death and no longer either cause or suffer death. This is the message which is given by the number 6.

The number 9 which is sometimes called the ninth path of the ECK is the pure essence of the spirit current which flows out of the SUGMAD and which is called the ECK, or the audible life stream. It is primarily the number of initiation for the one who is initiated has manifested the divine through the initiation in each of the three worlds from the physical through the Atma and in the first three of the pure worlds.

Every step by which we evolve from number 0 to the next step is an initiation of some sort or other. But after each three such minor steps there is a major initiation in ECK which when passed admits us into the new cycle and a new realm of consciousness. At each minor initiation we must face the ego, the personality, in ourselves, but at each major initiation we must face ourselves in the Atma Sarup (Soul body). This is why we are working in the field of threes, within the works of ECKANKAR.

While number 9 has always been considered the number of mystery, it is said to embody the power of silence or that sacred hush in which all activity is swallowed up in the initiation of new life. It is that darkness just before the dawn; the magnetic thrill as the sun drops below the horizon in the evening; the hush before the storm, or the pause at the turn of the tide.

Some ECK Masters like Apollonius of Tyana, in the first century A.D., understood the importance of 9 as a number. He required his disciples to strictly observe the 9th hour of the day and also he forbade his followers to mention the number 9 aloud. He said that the number must be passed over in silence, because it contained the great secrets of the initiate, the power which fructifies the earth, the mysteries of the secret fire, the universal key of languages and the second sight from which evil doers cannot remain concealed.

When number 9 was met with in their calculations it was passed over in silence, and a deep obeisance was made as a recognition of its sacred character. This, of course, was but a ceremony intended to impress upon the minds of the neophytes the great importance of initiation, its sacredness and the folly and danger of even speaking lightly concerning its mysteries.

His teachings of the number 9 is agreed upon for the mystic 9th hour, both as a period of the day, and as a period of Soul's evolution, is a cycle of most sacred and mysterious importance. At high noon all the forces of life are focused on the physical plane, hence great activity is going on in the physical body. This is the best time to eat a hearty meal, for as the sun has its greatest power in nature at high noon, so it is in man's body. Noon is also the best time to send out spiritual blessings to the world upon the physical plane, since it is the time of greatest activity and impressionability. From noon until 3 p.m., or during the 9th hour, should be a time of quiet rest and digestion, both of the physical food taken at noon, and the spiritual forces impressed on the physical body during the contemplative period.

The cat was in ancient times considered to be a sacred figure especially in the Egyptian religion mainly because it has the habit of curling up in a circle with its tail around its head, which was representative of the symbol of zero. As the naught, or zero, contained within itself the life and power of the 9 digits, so the cat is said to have 9 lives. The term lives however was originally not taken in its literal sense, but as referred to the 9 manifestations of the ECK current represented in the 9 digits.

The truth of this statement can be verified by the strange black cat which appeared in my early life, which was known as Jadoo. Its name means black magic in the eastern vernacular, and was one of those entities established to watch over me, and guard my person from attacks by either human or astral entities. The story of this relationship between a boy and his cat is told in my biography, "In My Soul, I Am Free," by Brad Steiger, Lancer books', 1968. And quite frequently the cat shows up wherever I might be. There are occasions when I am awakened out of a sound sleep to feel it jumping on the bed and curling up beside me. It's only natural to reach down to stroke its head to touch only emptiness and realize it came only in the spirit form. Other times I'd feel it rub against my leg while at work, and looking down see nothing with the physical eyes, only to realize that it died years ago. Then again it does appear occasionally in the physical to prove that it is really still around and protecting me.

The number 9 is the sun-force and should be revered as that which uplifts the individual through the higher initiation. If one learns to keep himself in silence concerning his spiritual unfoldment he finds at this point a quickening of his inner self. If he does not there is a danger of losing such spiritual advancement. For the babbler soon finds himself plunged into troubles and tests for which he is unprepared, and will wonder at his uncommon run of bad luck. The only way of finding wisdom and happiness is through silence. It is soon learned when he has developed the discipline of silence that he shall have knowledge and wisdom at his command, and that he shall pass the 9th initiation.

It is here that the Council of the Nine holds its court. It is a group of nine ECK Masters who have been appointed to take care of the affairs of the lower worlds, in every aspect from the sciences to religions. These are called the nine wisdoms and these Masters are in charge of them. It is only the advanced Souls who are able to study under these particular ECK Masters.

The number 12 is the number of completion or perfection through the initiation into the highest plane, that of the SUGMAD, the Ocean of Love and Mercy. The initiated Soul now stands forth as a responsible co-worker with the Supreme Deity. As the supreme initiate he must take his place with the adepts of the Ancient Order of the Vairagi in the guardianship of the beings and entities throughout the worlds of God. He has now the capability to voluntarily give a great love and compassion to the worlds, and take over the burden of the world's suffering and aid in its redemption.

A book of the mystical meaning of numbers could be written, however we are only concerned here with those which are connected with the ECK-Vidya. The number 12 being the great cycle takes in all the threes which are the inner cycles. It is also the beginning of the greater cycles which end in the number 60. It also represents the active principle of all life manifestations. Just as the 12 recurs again and again in its multiples, each 12 symbolizes a cycle of evolution and experience throughout the cycles of evolution on its journey of unfoldment, its great cycle of necessity. Just as each time a 12 is reached, its value is raised by the power of its new digit, 24, 48, 36, etc., while the greater cycles are indicated by the addition of 60, through 1200 and even beyond that.

Soul in Its journey passes through its minor incarnations, each dominated by a special phase of development compared to an added cycle of 12.

Just as the individual passes through the minor and major incarnations or cycles, so humanity as a whole passes through the minor cycles of unfoldment corresponding to the digits and then has its decisive or major cycles in which a perfect manifestation of the divine man, of the Godman, which is number 12, is expressed in the world in the person of the Mahanta, the living ECK Master. While the periodic falling away from the previous religious teachings and principles among the races and nations may seem like a lapse and a return to the selfish principle that force is right, still such periods of war and barbarism are but the burning up of the chaff of the old cycle, or the indrawing of the digits into the number 12.

The Mahanta, the living ECK Master, is the embodiment and expression of the SUGMAD, which is the perfection and completion of the number 12. He brings into the world a new cycle or the cycle of 12 of the manifested truth which the nations of the world cycle must unfold and manifest to the best of their ability with his spiritual help. Thus while the Mahanta, the living ECK

Master is perfect and complete, as the number 12 is perfect and complete, still he comes again with an added digit. This is why no religion, nation, society or individual can really progress while they cling to the traditions of the past. Each great cycle of 12 is a new period of starting over again which can be developed only through the light of the Mahanta, the living ECK Master, in the number 12 that manifests through the inspired teachings of any particular age, in the terms of its race thought and its advanced spiritual discoveries.

The sacred word here is the word HU. It represents the SUGMAD and therefore expresses all that can be said about the great cycle which is represented by the number 12. This is the cycle of the Lhokhor which is given in the earlier part of this book describing the 12th year of spiritual growth of man.

The number 60 is another important number in the ECK-Vidya works. It is represented by a wheel called the wheel of life, or the wheel of fortune. It is that which actually is called the heart of the SUGMAD, the dwelling place of the unknown deity. It is here that the Mahanta, the living ECK Master is born and comes forth upon the earth as the Godman.

This is the number 12 multiplied five times which brings into life the greatest of all avatars, and who uplifts mankind with his presence in the world. This is the works of ECK, which springs from the heart of the SUGMAD, the esoteric teachings from which other religions and philosophies are the offsprings, and the foundation essence of all life.

The esoteric teachings of ECK are that after Its involution into the matter worlds, the evolution of each Soul takes place along a spiral pathway within a series of concentric spheres of different densities, whose centers are all with the physical shell, corresponding with the concentric globes forming the planet chains, the finer interpenetrating the denser spheres.

All this the ECK Master knows in his ECK-Vidya reading of any chela who makes the request for one. When Soul has manifested the most essential and characteristic possibilities of the smallest, innermost and densest spheres of the aura, it breaks through that shell which confines it and follows the spiraling path upward into a larger sphere of consciousness. This is the number 60 orbit of evolution, which Soul takes after leaving the first of the number 12 cycles. It is then moving beyond the state of perfection, which has been found only to be another step on the road to Godhood.

Odd numbers are considered sacred because when we attempt to divide them into equal parts they leave the number 3 standing unaffected between themselves and the Supreme Deity. Thus they reveal the Highest of the High in the midst of ITS works. The even numbers can be divided into two equal parts without revealing the 1 God in their midst. Therefore even numbers can always be measured by a pair of opposites while the odd numbers cannot be.

While number 1 is the manifestation of the unmanifested, it in its own way represents the beginning of life. Yet the number 3 is that which is the start toward the perfection of life, and few persons can find himself ready for the higher truths until he has passed the third initiation in ECKANKAR. While number 1 may be the law it is the physical law which is yet to be manifested, and at the same time the number 3 is the spiritual law, rather the beginning of the spiritual disciplines which the higher law demands of its disciples.

This is why the number 60 is almost impossible to talk about in terms of the written word, because so few know what it means, and can grasp whatever words can be said about it. It is here that we learn that one is working with the number 12 multiplied by five that brings the cycles up to 60. This makes number 5 somewhat important in the sacred numbers considered by the ECK Masters. The 5 in the psychic worlds is of importance to the physical and mental systems of man. It represents the sympathetic nervous system and the intuitive areas. It is also the balance within man's own realm of life, ready to move forward into the higher realms. The five points of the star, the five fingers or toes, the five repetitions of the secret word of the initiation of the five planes, the five virtues, contentment, compassion, piety, patience and morality. The five deadly passions of the mind are lust, anger greed, attachment, and vanity.

The number 5 and its symbol which is the pentacle, reminds man that he is both human and divine; that he stands to the lower kingdom as a god to bless or curse in proportion to the degree which he finds a balance and meters out a just weight to all things. Hence at the entrance into the higher worlds stands the injunction for man to know himself, in which he enters in the state of Self-Realization on the 5th plane which is the Soul plane.

Here man is blessed in knowing his divine powers and his human

143

limitations, and earnestly gathers up all that he finds in the lower worlds and the lower self to be cast into the secret fires of ECK to be purified and harmonized to be brought to a perfect balance in himself. Thus he can come to truly know himself and enter into the first enlightenment of Self-Realization.

Thus we find that the number 60 is the animating principle of life and recognizing that it is the same creative principle which has given It enlightenment, Soul can set aside all which It has gathered as truth up to this point and let Itself be, in the arms of the Almighty Being. There is hardly anything else that It can do except this. Life manifests itself in the lap of the elements, and rebuilds the constitution of the kingdom of Soul in a high world which is completely beyond the imagination of the average man.

The number 60 is that which is in relationship with all things in all universes, and none can escape it. It can multiply itself or it can decrease itself, but there is little need in any case for it to do so for the unity of the Supreme Being manifests the sums ITSELF up in the unity of all and every being, entity and things in all ITS worlds.

The gate of heaven is to the East, although this has nothing to do with the geographical position, except we face the East in contemplation. This is the 6th gate, and has something to do with the number 6 in the field of sacred numbers. Now we also find that without will and determination to reach the ultimate goal of God we become the fixed results of cause and effect in its determined order. Will is the directing faculty of intelligent forces for the conciliation of the liberty of persons with the necessity of things. Power is the wise use of the will which enlists finality itself in the accomplishment of the ECK Masters.

Therefore we find a considerable difference in the human will and divine will. The human will is made up generally of the traits that consist of stubbornness and hard fisted decisions that are concerned with greed, anger, lust and vanity, as well as attachment. At the same time the divine will is consisted of those opposite virtues which make up the positive side of the individual. The human will is the will of the Kal (negative) power and the divine will is the will of the ECK (positive) power. Either one can use the individual. It is up to him to allow either of them to fill his consciousness.

This is all concerned with the number 6, with its six pointed star. The number 7 which is connected up with the seventh initiation is that by which the divine law manifests itself in seven major aspects in the worlds of God. We can mainly find it in the manifestation in the races of man, and in man himself. Like the planetary chain and the race of men, man himself is a 7 fold being, composed of the 3 and 4 numbers, within the lower worlds. It is the Bhakti initiation which is that of love, and whenever anyone enters into it, they symbolically give up everything in their physical and mental lives, as well as their spiritual.

Generally speaking the numbers before the number 10, and including it has something to do with the lower worlds; at least a connecting up with spiritual and the psychic regions. But after one has passed the first initiations and entered into the 9th or 10th he finds the great experience — overcoming all things in his life and there is no turning back; this is also true at the fifth and sixth initiations but not in the intensity as those in the higher numbers.

Number 8 is the number of evolution and is connected with the spiral motion of cycles. It is the balance in which Soul is weighed to see if It should be returned to the lower worlds for more experience and perfection, if there is any karma left to be rid of before going on to the higher planes.

Number 10 was called the ending of the decimal system by the ancients because they did not go any further. But actually it is the fountain of life, or the stream of ECK flowing forever throughout the worlds of God. Number 11 is the number of instruction, either in the position of being instructed in the arts of the ancient wisdoms, or being the Master who gives the instructions.

CHAPTER 10

THE KEY TO THE ECK-VIDYA SYMBOLS

No one can go far in the study of the spiritual works of ECKANKAR especially with the ECK-Vidya without becoming aware of the importance of symbols, for symbols are the language of the mysteries and of that greatest of all mysteries the psychic nature of man.

While it is true that we are not interested mainly in the psychic side of man, it is something which those concerned with the ECK-Vidya should know about and have well understood within their own minds, and hearts.

It is said there are over one thousand distinct languages recognized by linguists, more than a hundred auxiliary languages like Esperanto and basic English, not to mention the dead languages, slang, and the technical lingo of various trades and professions. Little wonder then that man has dreamed and yearned for a universal language, a system of communication that could reach intact from the remote past into the incalculable future and speak distinctly and personally to those who are traveling the varied paths to God.

Besides symbols we find that throughout the whole of the sacred works of any religion there are key words which represent the secret meaning of esoteric understanding. For example the word Solomon means 'man of the sun.' Other words definitely have meaning so that when one finds the whole key to the language of the spirit, not that of the psychic, he can certainly see new meanings.

First, the secrets of the psychic sciences, that is the science of the unrevealed, show that there is, in fact, a different language and the words of that language are symbols in form. It is the universal language between man and the Kal, the universal god of the lower worlds, and between man and nature, and between the conscious and subconscious factors of the mind itself. On the other hand the second part is that which is the language of the illuminated.

However, we shall proceed with the consideration of symbols in general and of certain key symbols in particular. Chief among the latter are those which man has derived from nature: the circle, triangle, cross and cube. There are others of course which will be discussed in this chapter.

The circle represents unity, completeness, the integrated whole and has powerful psychic implications as to its use in the various arts. By the means of the principle embodied in this symbol, man unites his finite human consciousness with the forces of the Infinite for good or evil. By tradition, the witch and the ceremonial magician perform their rituals with a clearly definite magic circle which serves the dual purpose of concentrating psychic energy for a specific purpose within the circle and of preventing useful, but possibly harmful, energies from invading the circle and assaulting the practitioner.

It is the symbol of the magician's own consciousness and the limits he has set to a specific ritual or operation. The drawing of the circle within itself, is no protection, but the state of mind induced and symbolized by the performance, the assurance and direction it gives to the magician, is a very real factor indeed.

The ancients considered the circle as God, the center of which represents boundless space and limitless time in eternity. It marks off the space in which creation takes place or the circle formed by the downpouring of the creative force in the psychic worlds. Every circle is a unity and every unit is or may be expressed by the circle. There are no straight lines in nature. Nature seems to run in circles, curves, spirals, arcs and whorls. The branches of trees appear to curve, as well as flower stems. Time also is curved, the cells of the body are circular, the skull domed, the foot arched, and other parts of the body are either cylindrical, tubular or circular. Persistent thinking upon this including the moon and sun as disks, the zodiac also, will open the doors to the unknown mysteries of the psychic worlds.

The circle is formed by a serpent, the supposed symbol of life and knowledge, swallowing its tail, symbolizing unending life and immortality. But the symbol means far more than the cycle of time, for it also symbolizes the source of creation in the lower worlds, the womb of nature, from which the future man proceeds, even the fetus in the womb being curved upon itself in a circular fashion.

The manifestation of the creative force in the physical world in its aspect as sex is a most potent factor in man's evolution, spiritual as well as physical. In fact upon its right understanding rests the destiny of mankind on this planet. Only by the power of the ECK can man meet and conquer all that comes to him in his manifestation and out of the blind forces of sex can he create a new life for himself and all concerned.

The cube is the square which by extension becomes the cube, a six-sided, equal-faceted symbol of truth. It is this cube or stone, which has become the cornerstone of the temple of human consciousness. Falsehood crumples and gives way to time. It is only truth which can endure the pressures of time and change. It is for this reason that most altars have a solid square or rectangular form.

The cube unfolded forms a cross. The meaning of symbology is that the cube represents the undeveloped man; regardless of whether it is in form of the cross or the cube. It is the mere personality which has within itself the potentialities of the divine man. But to manifest these potentialities the ECK must be born in the spiritual consciousness, or the heart, and awakened and unfolded.

In ancient times the cross was worn as a talisman against evil. It was placed upon the breast of the dead after embalmment. The Swastika or Thor's Hammer, another form of the balanced cross, is commonly worn as a talisman. In the light of the neophyte it is supposed to bring about purification, adjustment and balance by blows from its whirling ends or by the hard knocks of karma, hence its name the Hammer of Thor.

No struggle, of all the myriad bitter conflicts to engage mankind, has been more persistent and universal than the struggle to discover, establish and uphold truth. The diamond like the cross and the cube, is related to the physical world and man's human experience. It represents divine power brought to bear upon the material conditions. Intuition, clairvoyance, inspiration are faculties of the higher mind whereby light is reflected as from a flawless diamond.

In form the diamond is a double or reversed triangle and the triangle itself represents spirit when the apex is uppermost and

149

matter, when the apex is reversed. The seal of Solomon is formed by superimposing two equilateral triangles so as to form a six pointed star, a powerful symbol in magic. It symbolizes the great dualistic forces in nature which, together with an underlying cosmic force unity, form the mysterious trinity or triad on which every cosmogony and theogony is based.

The upward-pointing triangle, of which the great Pyramid is an architectural example, symbolizes spirit, of which the elementary manifestation is fire. If you strike a match or light a candle and observe the flame it's found the flame rises. This is a quality which is representative of spirit and of all things spiritual, that may be uplifting and noble.

The downward-pointing triangle is related to the element of water and that vast, submerged area we call the subconscious mind. As water flows downward and seeks its own level, so ideas and impressions are received by the subconscious mind. As the ocean is unexplored, full of mysteries and wonders, rich in resources and of immense psychic power, we find that each counterpart of the triangle is a power in its own right.

The triangle symbolizes affinity and harmony, for each of those elements combined within it, water, fire and air, stand in triangular relationship and its relationship in the affairs of man, mind and spirit, in similar placement are said to be the favorable aspects of life and ECK. Yet it is often thought of as the symbol of the triune Godhead. But all manifestations of that Godhead must contain a reflection of the triangle: the inner reality, the outer manifestation, and the life force which unites the dual forces.

Next we find the five-pointed star which is often called the pentacle of the magicians. The mystic wand said to have been used by Moses and Aaron and all initiates was described as a rod with a 5-pointed star at its end. It is used in all magical rites both black and white and is noted that to this magic symbol of the pentacle every elemental force must bow. Man himself is this pentacle, for with his hands out-stretched, his feet spread and his head erect, he forms the 5-pointed star.

The flames, which are said to issue from the 5 points of the pentacle on the end of the wand are the powers inherent in the perfected body, the glorious robe of man's strength. For when the five senses of men are illuminated by the divine fire of the ECK, they radiate the spiritual powers by which he can perform all the miracles of the true magician. The mystical significance of this symbol is that as man, through his spiritual development, lifts up the fiery force of the Kundalini power which functions through the spinal column (the rod), and with it flaming forth from his five extremities and illuminating his five senses (the pentacle) on all planes he indeed becomes a magician capable of performing either white or black magic. The flaming pentacle also represents man's uplifted hand with his magnetic force streaming from his five fingers. The flaming pentacle is but another version of the truth symbolized by the parable of the 5 wise virgins who kept their lamps trimmed and burning, while the pentacle reversed refers to the 5 foolish virgins who could not enter in.

The pentacle in reversal, the 1 point down and the two points up, is a symbol of black magic, for this places man's head and hands on the ground and his feet in the air. This focuses his 5 powers downward on the lower planes; that he is proceeding downward instead of evolving upward, using his head to scheme and his hands to pull at whatever possible at the expense of others, instead of blessing and uplifting all.

The reversal of the symbol is intentionally done by the black magicians. No black magician seeking merely for phenomena or personal power has ever or can ever truly enter into man's divine heritage. All the sin, suffering, disease, antagonism and misery manifested in the world today results from man's reversal of the pentacle, of himself and his powers.

The symbol of the pentacle is to show that man is both human and divine; that he stands at the top of the lower kingdom as a minor god, to bless or curse in proportion to the degree to which he finds a just balance and will mete out just weights to all things within the lower kingdoms.

Bells are another symbol which is important to the ECK-Vidya. For example its sound is a symbol of creative power. Since it is in a hanging position, it partakes of the mystic significance of all objects which are suspended between heaven and earth. It is related, by its shape to the vault and consequently, to the heavens.

The tolling bell is both a mark of death and a defense against evil. They have been used for social, ritual and magical purposes from time immemorial. In the pagan temple of antiquity the bell's outer shell was regarded as female and the clapper as the male. The use of bells in the rites of religions of the world, stems from their early use in magic. They were rung by the Chinese to summon rain, by the Tyrolese to protect the harvest. Even bells attached to domestic animals, such as the pack horses, donkeys, burros, had and still have in some parts of the world, the additional function of affording protection against evil spirits. In modern Italy they are worn by horses and cattle as a defense against the Evil Eye.

Bells, of course, represent the ECK, the audible life stream, yet the tinkling of bells is the representative sound for the causal plane, which is the plane of memory. Here is where the memories, karmic patterns and akashic records are stored in the lower worlds; that is the astral and physical planes. It is above the time track of the physical worlds and when one reaches this area he can read the records of the individual but only for the first three planes. The full reading of the individual Soul must be done from the fifth world, that of the Atma Sarup.

The chime hours in the ancient times attached to bells and bell ringing were particularly at the time of 3, 6, 9 and 12, which are established as the mystical numbers of the ECK-Vidya. But it's found that those born during these particular hours are not only blessed with second sight but have great wisdom.

The Tisra Til, or the spiritual eye, is another symbol of interest to those in the works of ECKANKAR. The single eye has always been of deep concern to the seekers of the heavenly illumination. If the eye becomes single its owner must surrender all of himself to the ECK, the spiritual power, or what is known in ECK-ANKAR, as the Mahanta, the living ECK Master.

This is sometimes called the third eye, often the all-seeing eye of God. This is also connected in a way with the zero or naught spoken of in the first part of this chapter. The evil eye is another part of the sightless eye which can influence and harm people. Anyone traveling through the countryside of Pennsylvania, or in the eastern part of Europe will find certain figures and hexes painted on walls to ward off those who would do harm to them and their farm animals.

This is the four petalled center in the chakra which is located between the eyebrows, at which point the ECK Master teaches us to concentrate all attention when we do the spiritual exercises of ECK. This third eye is also called the Shiva-netra, the eye of Shiva. It is also the Nukti-i-saveda the black point in the circle, the naught. In the works of ECK, all concentration is begun at this point and held there, until ready to go higher. All the lower centers of chakras used in the yoga systems are disregarded. This is one of the fundamental differences between the system of the ECK Masters and that of all yogis, following the Patanjali method. The ECK works actually begin its work where all other systems leave off. For few persons, other than the ECKists, if any, go above this chakra. While the ECK Masters know of the lower chakras, they disregard them, knowing that they are unimportant.

The mandala is another symbol which is sometimes used in the ECK-Vidya. This is a Hindu term for a circle. It is kind of an emblem, in the form of a ritual geometric diagram, sometimes corresponding to a specific, divine attribute or some form of enchantment which is given visual expression.

The mandalas are found all over the Orient, and in some of the western countries today. They are always a means toward contemplation and concentration, as an aid in inducing certain mental states and in encouraging the spirit to move forward along its path of evolution from the biological to the geometric, from the realm of corporeal forms to the spiritual.

The mandala is not only painted or drawn, but is also actually built in three dimensions for some festivals. Sometimes it's a mental image which may be built up in the imagination only by the ECK Masters. It is said that no one mandala is the same as another. All are different because each is a projected image of the psychic condition of its author, or in other words, an expression of the modification brought by this psychic contents to the traditional idea of the mandala. It is a synthesis of a traditional structure plus free interpretation. Its basic components are geometric figures, counterbalanced and concentric. It has been said that the mandala is always squaring the circle.

Some mandalas which counterbalance not only enclosed figures within the circle but numbers arranged in geometric discontinuity: for instance, four points, then five, then three, and then identified with them are the cardinal points of astrology, the elements and colors as well as symbols.

In the ancient days especially in China each family of nobility as well as the ruler of the country, had their own mandalas made up in the same manner as the coat of arms is for many of the western families. In fact different families wore their own particular mandala on their robes, or had it displayed over the doorway of their palaces.

The juxtaposition of the circle, triangle and the square, the equivalents of the numbers one and ten; three, and four and seven plays a fundamental role in the most classic and authentic of oriental mandalas. Even though the mandala always alludes to the concept of the center, never actually depicting it visually but suggesting it by means of the concentricity of the figures, at the same time it exemplifies the obstacles in the way of achieving and assimilating the center. In this way, the mandala fulfills its function as an aid to the individual in his efforts to regroup all that is dispersed around a single axis, the concept of the center, and again though not always visible to the eye, but only to the mind.

The Eagle is another symbol of interest to the ECK student. It represents a symbol of height, of the sun, as well as the spirit of the individual, and of the spiritual principles in general. The eagle is a bird living in the full light of the sun and it is considered to be luminous in its essence, and to share in the elements of air and fire. Its opposite is the owl, the bird of darkness, and death. Since it is identified with the sun and with the idea of male activity it also symbolizes the masculine principle, and that which must be the equivalent of the feminine principle. It is characterized by its daring flight, its speed, its close association with thunder and fire. It also signifies the rhythm of heroic nobility and has always been considered the symbol also of the ruler, the king of the element of air and fire.

From the Far East to Northern Europe, the eagle is the bird associated with the gods of power and war. It is the equivalent in the air as the lion is on earth. According to the Vedic tradition, it is also important as a messenger, being the bearer of the soma from Indra. In the Sarmatian arts, the eagle is the emblem of the thunderbolt and of warlike endeavor. In all Oriental art it is often shown fighting, but in the pre-Columbian days in South America its symbolism was to signify the struggle between the spiritual and celestial principles and the lower world. The same symbolism also occurs in the Romanesque art.

In ancient Syria, in an identification rite, the eagle with human arms symbolized sun worship which was the religion of the day in that particular country. It also had another duty to conduct Souls to immortality, over the border of death to heaven. Similarly, in

Christianity, the eagle plays the role of spirit of prophecy in general; it has been also identified more exactly as the eagle's flight, because of its swiftness, rather than the bird itself, with prayer rising to the heavens, and grace descending upon mortal man.

Among the Greeks it acquired a particular meaning, more allegorical than properly symbolic in nature, in connection with the rape of Ganymede. More generally speaking, it was believed to fly higher than any other bird, and was regarded as the most apt expression of divine majesty. The connection between the eagle and the thunderbolt, already mentioned, is confirmed in Macedonian coinage and in the Roman signum, a type of coin in ancient Rome. The ability to fly and fight, to rise so as to dominate and destroy the baser forces, is without doubt the essential characteristic of all the eagle symbolism.

On the Roman coins the eagle was impressed as the symbol of imperial power and of the legionary strength. The two-headed eagle of the Austrian rulers, and the German Kaisers before World War I, were usually depicted as the double strength of the Imperial power. Often this type eagle was of great mystical significance: red and white.

In many of the emblems portraying the eagle, the symbols and allegories show it carrying a victim. This is always an allusion to the sacrifice of lower beings, forces, instincts and to the victory of the higher powers. Dante even called the eagle the bird of God, Jung referred to it in mystical terms, and others prominent in history and religion have used the eagle for some symbolism of a sort.

The Door is another symbol which the ECK-Vidya reader is interested in and makes reference to occasionally. In most spiritual arts it is a feminine symbol, but the ECKist never looks at it in this manner. The Door is an opening into a better world, it is that which one can see through into the garden of God. It is often referred to as the Door of Soul, which opens inwardly, never outward. When one can get a glimpse through the Door into inner worlds and see the light illuminating the garden of beauty there, and the wonderful music of the SUGMAD which is issuing forth from it he has no other desire than to enter therein and dwell there forever.

Blood is another symbol which most of those who are

155

interested in the mantic sciences find of value. The symbolism of the blood is in its color of red because this can represent love, or violence. It depends on the color of the blood, light red or pink represents love, while deep, dark red is that of violence. We find the perfect symbol of sacrifice in spilt blood. All liquid substances, milk, honey and wine, which were offered up in antiquity to the dead, to spirits and to gods, were images of blood, the precious offering of all things which could be offered.

Sacrificial blood was obtained from sheep, the hog and the bull in classical times, and from human sacrifices among the Asians, and the Mayans of Mexico and Central America, also the Africans and Indians of North America. The blood was to appease the powers and ward off the most severe troubles which might befall those who made the sacrifice.

The blood has a special chemistry which will, when spilt in violence, draw to its spot upon the floor or earth demons, ghosts and all the invisible elements which are harmful to man. They will abide here until either the changing of the soil or decay of the floor by rot or some other natural way, or by the means of exorcism, which is to cast out an evil spirit, by some spiritual authority.

Blood revenge by clans and families in old Europe, and other places in the world has only released a large number of wicked spirits and demons that often take possession of the descendants of those quarreling families. This is true especially of those families who continue to live in the same building, house or castle where murders were committed. Many of the old estates in the Transylvania mountains in Hungary have been said to have the descendants of fighting clans living under the influence of the malignant discarnate entities. It is also said this is true of certain areas in Germany, Scotland and other European countries.

The Drums are a symbol of primordial sound, and a vehicle for the word, for tradition and for magic. With the aid of drums, the shamans, a certain sect of magicians, can induce a state of ecstasy. It is not only the rhythm, and the timbre which are important in the symbolism of the primitive drum, but since it's supposedly made of the wood of the Tree of the World, the mystic sense of the ladder also refers to it. According to musical experts, the drum is, of all musical instruments, the most pregnant with mystic ideas.

It is associated with the heart in Africa. In the most primitive cultures, including the Voodoo religion, as in the most advanced, it is equated with the sacrificial altar and acts as a mediator between heaven and earth. However, with its bowl-shape and its skin, it corresponds more properly with the symbolism of the earth element. However, the three essential shapes of the drum are: the drum in the form of an hour-glass, symbolizing inversion and the relationship between the two worlds, the upper and lower; the round drum, as an image of the world; and the barrel-shaped, associated with thunder and lightning.

The tree is one of the most essential traditional symbols. But very often the symbolic tree is of no particular genus, although some trees have been singled out of one or another species as the tree of life, or the sacred tree to singular and particular religious sects. The oak was sacred to the Celts; the ash to the Scandinavian peoples; the lime tree to the German tribes; the fig tree to the Indus in India.

There were many mythological associations between the ancient gods and trees, for example there was Osiris and the cedar; Jupiter and the Oak; Apollo and the laurel, and Attis and the pine. At its best in symbology the tree denotes the life of the cosmos: its consistence, growth, proliferation, generative and regenerative processes. It stands for inexhaustible life, and is equivalent to a symbol of immortality. The concept of life without death stands for absolute reality and, consequently, the tree becomes a symbol of this absolute reality, that is, of the center of the world. Because a tree has a long, vertical shape, the center of the world symbolism is expressed in terms of a world axis.

The tree with its roots underground and its branches rising to the sky symbolizes an upward trend and is therefore related to other symbols, such as the ladder and the mountain, which stand for the general relationship between the three lower worlds. Clearly the tree can only be the axis linking the worlds if it stands in the center of the cosmos they constitute. It is interesting to note that the worlds of tree-symbolism reflect the three main portions of the structure of the tree: roots, trunk and foliage. Within the general significance of the tree as world-axis and as a symbol of the inexhaustible life-process, growth and development, different mythologies and folklores have different shades of meaning. Some of these are merely aspects of the basic symbolism, but others are of a subtlety which gives further enrichment to the symbol.

At the primitive level there is the Tree of Life and the Tree of Death, a duality which is well known in the psychic worlds. Others know the tree as the symbolism of the cosmic tree and the tree of the knowledge of good and evil; but the two trees are merely two different representations of the same idea. In India the huge banyan tree is sacred because Buddha received his enlightenment under such a species of tree. There is also a ceremony in India called the tree marriage in which a man or woman is symbolically married to a tree.

The tree is frequently related to the rock or mountain on which it grows. On the other hand the tree of life, as found in the celestial Jerusalem, bears twelve fruits, or sun shapes. In many images, the sun, the moon and the stars are associated with the tree, stressing its cosmic and astral character. There is a triple tree, in India, with three suns and the image of their Hindu trinity. In China, there is a tree with the twelve suns of the zodiac. Other types of trees have been the tree of knowledge and the sea tree.

The wheel is a symbol, wide in scope, much used in ornamental arts, in certain forms of Oriental religions, and known quite well in the ECK-Vidya, the ancient science of prophecy.

One of the elementary forms of the wheel-symbolism consists of the sun as a wheel and of ornamental wheels as solar emblems. The concept of the sun as a wheel was one of the most widespread notions of antiquity. The idea of the sun as a two-wheeled chariot is not far removed from this idea. The same ideas can be found among the Aryans and also among the Semites. Given the symbolic significance of the sun as a source of light which stands for intelligence and of spiritual illumination, it is easy to understand why the Buddhist doctrine of the solar wheel has been so widely admired.

There have been all types of wheels known: the Catherine wheel, wheels of fire, wheels of fortune, wheels of the year, solar wheels, and zodiac wheels, all rooted in what was first known as the sun, described as the fiery wheel by the ancients.

The swastika is another type of wheel, while the lotus flower is considered by some to be an emblem of the wheel. There is also the emblems of the Chinese which are the wheel of law, truth and life. The Chinese used it as a form of good luck in Buddhism and it illustrates the way of escape from the illusory world and from the illusions and the way towards the center of all things.

The wheel of fortune is an allegory which is a general symbolism of the wheel. Based upon the symbolism of number 2, it expresses the equilibrium of the contrary forces of contraction and expansion, the principle of polarity. It is a part of the symbolism of life, and also a part of the symbolism of gambling because it also represents chance.

The lion is the ancient symbol of gold, and often represented the sun-gods such as Mithras. In Egypt of the olden days it was believed that the lion presided over the annual floods of the Nile river, because the floods coincided with the entry of the sun into the zodiacal sign of Leo during the dog-days. The lion has been used for many symbols, for rulers and despots who believed themselves the king of their people, corresponding with the lion as the king of the beasts.

The king of the beasts also symbolized the earthly opponent of the eagle in the sky and the lord and master, or the possessor of strength of the masculine principle. During times in the ancient world one of the favorite sports was to match the lion and the bull in a death struggle. But the lion pertains to the element of earth and the symbolic winged lion to the element of fire. Both are the symbolism of continued struggle, solar light, morning, regal dignity and victory. The lion also became a symbolism to be associated with St. Mark in the Evangelists.

The mountain is attached to symbolism because it is equated with the inner loftiness of spirit, for it transposes the notion of ascent to the realm of Soul. Because of its great proportions the mountain became a symbol to the Chinese for the greatness and generosity of their emperor.

Some of the sacred mountains in mythology are, Sumeru of the Ural-Altaic people, Caf in Moslem mythology, a huge mountain which has a base of a single emerald called Sakhrat, Mount Meru of Hindu folklore which is said to be of gold and located at the North Pole and Himinbjor of the German peoples.

Mount Olympus which is a real mountain was and is of great fame as it was the supreme, celestial mountain which was the abode of the Greek gods. There are other mountains and mountain ranges which have been famous in mythology. The forbidding mountain ranges of the Andes, the Himalayans, and the Rockies have created legends which make those interested in spiritual matters feel that often there is truth in what the natives have had to say about them in relation to their mythologies.

The Pyramid is a symbolism which apparently has several contradictions. First, it is symbolic of the earth in its maternal aspect for the ancient Egyptians. When decorated with lights and other gaudy things for holidays it expresses the twofold idea of death and immortality, both associated with the great Mother of Nature.

Generally speaking the pyramid is a hollow mountain, the dwelling place for the spirits of the Pharoahs. Its square base represents the earth, while the apex is the starting point and finishing point of all things. The triangular shaped faces of the pyramid, symbolizes fire, divine revelation and the threefold principle of creation.

The thunderbolt, or lightning, is the symbolism of the celestial fire as an active force, terrible and swift to destroy. The examples of this in mythology is the thunderbolt of Parabrahman, and the fire ether of the Greeks, both symbols of the supreme creative power. The thunderbolt of the Tibetans represents power.

The thunderbolt is held to be the emblem of sovereignty. The winged thunderbolt expresses the ideas of power and speed. The three thunderbolts of Jupiter symbolize chance, destiny and providence, the forces that mold the future. In the majority of religions we find that the godhead is hidden from man's gaze, and then suddenly the lightning flash reveals him momentarily in all his active might. The image of the logos piercing the darkness is universal. The vajra of the Tibetan symbol for both the thunderbolt and diamond is also connected with the world axis, the action of the higher powers upon the lower.

Nine steps on the ladder is a symbolism of the nine steps or stages of the spiritual development of an ECKist, toward becoming a co-worker with God. These are set forth in more detail in the Shariyat-Ki-Sugmad. They are: (1) The stage of joy, in which you, the ECKist, develop your holy nature and discard wrong views. (2) The stage of Illumination, in which you attain perfection of patience or humility, and also the deepest introspective insight. (3) The stage of divine knowledge in which you achieve and realize the harmony of worldly truth and supreme truth. (4) The stage of perfection in which you receive the divine wisdom as your own. (5) The stage of perfection in which you receive the ability to save all beings. (6) The stage of perfection in which you realize that all things are false except the God nature of all creatures and things. (7) The stage in which you attain the ten holy powers and can create miracles with humility. (8) The stage of mastery of perfect realization in which you can preach the law to save all creatures. (9) The stage of perfection in which you can be supreme in all things, to create the higher miracles without the knowledge of people, accept karma and be with the living ECK Master to help in his work.

Symbols are generally the archetype of ideas which have been long implanted in the subconscious, and only show up in dreams, visions and sometimes in illusions. But they are important to the ECK-Vidya reader for when he sees the aura filled with certain symbols or can see symbols in the subconscious mind of the readee he knows what they are, and can tell the readee about them.

He also knows and understands when he is doing an ECK-Vidya reading, when symbols appear in the mind of the individual, in past lives and perhaps in the future lives. He is well aware of the problems which arise at times, and although only a few samples of symbols have been given here, anyone can start understanding his own thoughts and visions.

CHAPTER 11

THE FUTURE OF THE HUMAN RACE, EARTH AND OTHER PLANETS

The history which we study in school and in the higher institutions of learning is that which is known as popular history. Although popular history is good for the mind and it sometimes helps us to trace past incarnations for our individual selves, at the same time it is hardly anything in accord with cosmic history.

This is what we are mainly concerned with in this chapter, for cosmic history deals in the cycles of the subject in what are known as the manvantara, a cycle of cosmic time. The current manvantara embraces the Sat Yuga, the Golden Age, of what is known as the age of truth. The Golden Age which lasts 1,728,000 of our years is the first four-tenths of the entire manvantara.

This is followed by the Tretya Yuga, the second age or what we know as the Silver Age. It is one fourth less righteous and briefer than the Golden Age, enduring 1,296,000 of our years, which is three-tenths of the entire manvantara.

The Dwapara Yuga, which is the third age, of that known to us as the Copper Age, is supposedly a fourth less righteous than the preceding one and it lasts between 864,000 and 1 million years of our years, or two tenths of the entire cosmic cycle of the manvantara.

This is followed again by the Kali Yuga, the last yuga of the current manvantara. It is called the Iron Age or the Dark Age in which all is characterized by strife, discord, quarreling and contention. It is a fourth less righteous and briefer than the Dwapara Yuga, and supposedly lasts some 500,000 years which is one tenth of the entire manvantara. This is the age in which we are currently living and was supposedly to have started at midnight between the 17th and 18th of February, 3102, B.C.

Although I have given some data on the different ages of the earth and the lower worlds previously as designated by the various yugas just mentioned, it's time to talk about the doctrine of cycles which will clear up a large number of things which the student of the ECK-Vidya system has not yet found in the works of this particular way of prophecy.

The doctrine of cycles contains much vital information and many amazing solutions to the philosophical problems that have puzzled the western students of spiritual matters for centuries. The accumulated wisdom of the ages has been employed in the formulation of this basic doctrine which constitutes the solid foundation of cosmic and planetary chronology. It was considered very sacred and esoteric and was guarded in the secret chambers of the temple of antiquity and only revealed to the high initiates at the time of initiation into the mysteries.

It is in the doctrine of cycles that the seeker of truth will come across the hidden information which contains all the valuable data for which he might have spent a lifetime to find the answers to his questions. However it is beyond the scope of this chapter to enter into a deep explanation of the eternal progression of cycles, as it would take volumes to properly describe the sacred doctrine of cycles and do it justice. Besides the more profound parts of the doctrine are still kept secret by its exalted and wise ECK Masters who are the guardians of the Shariyat-Ki-Sugmad in the Golden Temples of Wisdom and revealed only during the higher initiations.

The doctrine of cycles, like any other esoteric doctrine, is based upon the Hermetic axiom of correspondence which is the fundamental principle in the psychic philosophy and which is "As above, so it is below. That which has been will return again. As in heaven, so on earth."

One wonders what kind of experience has been utilized in the formulation of these records of cycles. Documentary records of the epochal changes which have occured with our planet and others at regular intervals during the distant, past periods, the memory of which has passed into oblivion, have never been mentioned in ancient books or histories of antiquity. There is recorded in these doctrines of cycles the sinking of the continent of Lemuria in the depths of the Pacific Ocean and later Atlantis into the Atlantic Ocean. Other records of great events and cataclysms that are to come are there in these strange records.

The doctrine of cycles is built upon the same principle governing the functions of the universal laws which operate through an infinite series of wheels within wheels and cycles within cycles, all bound to the same center in the fashion of concentric circles. It builds its works in the periodical manifestation by taking into consideration natural facts, such as life and death, day and night, sleep and waking periods, the four seasons of the year, the four periods of human existence, such as birth, growth, youth and old age, which indicate the cycle motion and evolutionary and involutionary, or ascending and descending arcs in the revolving drama of existence.

The doctrine of reincarnation is also a part of these cycles, many minor cycles working within one major cycle, such as the 999 cycles of earthly lives, or incarnations, of a human being on our planet, which form the one major cycle of evolutionary life toward perfection.

The four cycles governing human life are the same that govern mineral life, vegetable and animal life. The same doctrine also takes into account many facts about the constellations and their influences, as well as the major planets within this universe. The relationship between the physical body of man and the universe is certainly strange in many ways, and the strangest is that the body of man contains every piece of element and such as that which is within the universe.

The doctrine of cycles is a revelation of immense value to the truth seeker for it demonstrates the depths of the mysteries of life. We have gone into the cycles of life and into the years in another chapter but here we are talking about the succession of manifestations of the cosmic days and nights, known as the Maha Kalpas, Maha Manvantaras and the Pralayas. But these are concerned with billions of years which staggers the mind of the individual, so it isn't much use to go into these except to say that the cosmic day and night of the SUGMAD is equal to about three billion years. This means when the worlds of this material universe are destroyed and night sets in until the SUGMAD re-establishes the lower planes again for inhabitants, those Souls who have not been perfected and taken into heaven will sleep approximately this amount of time. Then they will be put back into this world once more to start all over again and be given an opportunity to meet the Mahanta, the living ECK Master, to make their way back into the kingdom of heaven again. The Pralaya is the time of the formation of a new universe in the bosom of the SUGMAD.

The various yugas as given here in the beginning of this chapter are concerned with several races that start with each age and eventually end with the finish of the dark age after which all imperfected Souls are taken into the Atma Lok (Soul plane) to sleep away until a new universe is formed for them once more. These races are the Polarian, or the first race, the Hyperborean, the Lemurian, the Atlantean, the Aryan, the Ulemans, the Shatikayas, the Arrians, the Kaishvits, the Heraclians, the Clemains, and the Freticrets.

These are the races which will and have occupied the earth world with the power of authority, either by conquest with arms or by diplomacy. At the present time we find that the Aryan race is in charge of this world, but this will change again within a few years to the Ulemans, which is a race that presently occupies the planet of Jupiter. This race will descend upon the earth and other planets throughout the solar system and occupy them, with absolute ruling power. This will happen around the year 2100. Their rule will last at least three hundred years before they are conquered by another race called the Shatikayas, which will come from one of the new continents that rises out of the depths of the Pacific Ocean in the same vicinity of the Lemurian continent which sunk thousands of years ago.

The Shatikayas will be a fierce warlike tribe, whose ancestory were the warrior tribes of old India. During an upheaval which will break up the land masses and sink parts of the world, including the coastal areas of China, United States, England completely and parts of Africa, Europe and others continents around the world, the new land mass called the Shatikaya continent will form and its civilization will begin.

This civilization will last about 1000 years. It will be one of the higher civilizations to have ever been on this earth planet. The development of the flying saucer type of plane will give this race the opportunity to cover Mars and a few other planets, and settle its people there. Their development in the many parts of sciences will increase the hold of the ruler-kings upon the peoples of these many lands. Revolts will take place but it's doubtful that any will ever succeed.

Gradually this race will weaken due to disease and intermarriage and it will resolve as a great race and be overcome by the Arrian race. The Arrians will sweep out of the arctic regions of the

166

northern world and conquer everything in its path. It will be a vigorous race which will take over about the year 3500 and spread beyond the rim of the world into Mars and Venus where their civilizations will be built and great trade routes developed.

The Arrians will be a hated race for they will practice cruelty upon the peoples of the worlds which they have conquered. They will have to put down bloody rebellions time and again; and their kings will be insecure on their thrones because of assassination plots which will come up frequently. Even their own sons and relatives will be in on these plots. They will rule approximately fifteen hundred years and then will be gone, by conquest from another race.

The new race will be from Mars. Its conquest of the earth and all the major planets of the constellation will be from taking advantage of the great cataclysm that will make this world and all the planets look like new ones. The majestic mountains will be flattened and the lands which we now travel as flat lands will be high rolling hills. New continents will spring up, new planets will appear in the skies and there will be new worlds to conquer. The planet of Mars will be one of the few which will not be affected by this disaster, which comes of two minor planets getting out of orbit and striking one another. This will release the gas pressures in the earth planet as well as other planets and the destruction will be great. The new race will be known as the Kaishvits, and will be in power for about five thousand years, then will vanish into time.

The next conqueror is the Heraclian race, a hearty race of people who will come up from the Southern areas, in the antarctic regions. This will be an improvement over the other races because these people will be a race of men who are fair in all their dealings, and will try to give justice to all that fall under their rule. They will try to intermingle with the conquered people, marry and set up business within an order of establishment. This will be around the year of 6025 and it will last as a civilization for at least five hundred to a thousand years. Most of the new arts and culture will be established in this time and will last for a long time before any succeeding people will ever take over and rebuild their civilizations on top of that which is known as the Heraclian race.

The Clemains race will follow this civilization. They will be a ruthless race which will try to destroy everything but will fail because the old traditions to which the people cling to cannot be destroyed. A new religion will come into being at this time, and it will consist of the priest-kings who like in the ancient times of this earth were God and man also, according to their own theory of divinity. They will kill off thousands of people because of their desire for loot, which will be jewels, gold and silver. But eventually all this will stop when they come to their senses that all the so-called treasures have been exhausted, and they will set out to conquer new worlds but will come to defeat by a new race from the world of Pluto called the Freticrets, who are almost as desperate and ruthless as themselves, but dealers in black magic.

It will be through black magic that the Freticrets will take control over all the nations on earth and most of the planets throughout the universe. The black magic which they will use will be so evil that it will eventually bring down the destruction of this universe and cause damage so badly that the worlds within this universe will be taken out of existence by fire and water.

This is at the time when the end of the Kali Yuga age will come about and it will end the period of those ages which man has gone through, for the age of the SUGMAD, which amounts up to about 5 or 6 million years. This is the end of the day of the SUGMAD, in the life of our solar system. It also includes the life of those psychic planes, the astral, causal, mental, and etheric or subconscious. This constitutes the entire period of the cosmic manifestation which will be followed by a period of equal duration, which is known as the cosmic night.

During this cosmic night there will be nothing in the lower worlds except chaos and darkness. All Souls which have not met the Mahanta, the living ECK Master and been taken into the heavenly worlds will sleep for the same duration of time. At the end of the cosmic night, the great building of the new worlds in the lower kingdom will begin again. While the Kal power (negative power) has had nothing to do except to roil and wander in the darkness of the cosmic night, it now begins again to start its duties in the lower worlds, that is testing and trying Souls to keep them from reaching perfection.

It is then that the individual Souls who have been returned to the lower worlds start over again in the Satya Yuga, the Golden Age. It may have to go through all the various ages once again before being established seriously on the path of ECK.

It was on Friday, September 23, 1949, that the end of the American monopoly over the atomic weapons came to an end.

The president of the United States announced that there was evidence that an atomic explosion had taken place somewhere in the Russian Soviet Union. This was the second explosion of its kind in the world, the other was at Hiroshima, August 6, 1945. It set the end of the world for all the human race. It began the dangerous road of power politics.

This put man at the awe-inspiring crossroads, the most decisive in his destiny. It put him up against some of the most ruthless power ever known in the history of this planet, and those who have taken the left-hand path of black magic. His right to life, prosperity, health and happiness went down the drain to the threats of a bottomless chasm of total annihilation.

Most people would rather not think about it, but life in the atomic age demands an exceptional expansion and growth of consciousness. But from what we have seen and known so far man has not been able to adjust and reform his ways and methods, not taking the opportunity to realize that he must reach moral maturity. He still behaves like a wild youth, feeling more arrogant by the possession of more formidable weapons. It's not unexpected that his behavior runs this way for the actual use of such a gigantic source of energy in warfare has bewildered and terrified the nations of the earth.

This is the great problem, for the preparation of the great nations for World War III has been going on since the finish of the Second World War. The Cold War only exists because it has been used for probing and as the time for the preparation for World War III. The brush wars and the infiltration of Russia into the varied countries, including Cuba, Egypt and other nations under the guise of helping them, as well as the building of huge fleet of ships is part of this building for another war. The war in Vietnam is a part of the United States' plans to prepare a front in Asia to keep from having to fight a war in the Pacific in her own back yard as we almost did during World War II. It is the same policy that Russia has used particularly in eastern Europe where she took over those countries of Poland, Czechoslovakia, Hungary, Bulgaria.

This is the result of the lesson learned during World War II when Hitler's legions rolled across neutral or conquered nations right onto Russian land with hardly a battle. Now Russia has established a defense belt which will keep any land armies away from direct contact with her frontiers. All fighting will be done on someone else's territory. This is the same reason by which her leaders established a Russian base in Cuba. This is the same reason by which the military leaders want to establish land bases in Asia as General MacArthur had advised, in Korea, Vietnam, Okinawa, the Phillipines and in Europe.

The propaganda is the dangerous tool in the hands of ruthless people. It is an instrument for the dissemination of falsehood, hatred and terror and one of the most wicked scourges of mankind. It should be totally abandoned because of its horrible and destructive effects and consequences. In the interest of peace, all nations must eliminate their propaganda departments and replace them with an information department which would broadcast nothing but the truth and would give out only friendship, peace, harmony and goodwill.

Propaganda distracts the attention of the people from concentrating on their own internal problems and causes them to deviate from their goal of progress and advancement. It sows seeds of discord, fear, suspicion and despair. It demoralizes nations and paralyzes their will and courage: creates tumult, confusion and chaos. This is what has happened to those nations who participated in propaganda in the cold and hot wars which we have had since World War II. This is a dangerous policy for any nation to use and those engaged in it will come to an untimely end, for there are no benefits and advantages, only bankruptcy and chaos which will precipitate war.

Propaganda, cold wars, hot wars and drugs are going to bring this last era of the Kali Yuga to a close with the largest amount of destruction that this world has ever known. It won't be as much of a big bang as that of the exhaustion of the people; the bankruptcy of their minds and bodies is going to have everything go out in the cosmic night of darkness with a whimper and a sobbing.

The drug problem is going to add to the fuel of the disaster. The manner in which drugs are being poured out upon the open market today for youth will find that the leadership of tomorrow is gone. The leaders will be those without feeling and compassion for the average man, and so much of the control of the masses will be done by drugs and minor narcotics. Tyranny and dictatorship will take place in the United States and many of the major countries of the world. In order to keep up their prestige and keep the minds of the people off the domestic problems, there will be propaganda and threats made by international leaders against one another, until one day about the first of the next century the troubles will really start. There will be the massacre of millions of innocent people in the destruction of many cities, and the infliction of the most ruthless indignities upon humanity, a cataclysm which would make the Mongol atrocities of the thirteenth century look insignificant. Besides all this the governments of the warring nations would waste approximately 400 billion dollars and the sight of mankind on this planet would be at an end.

Not only that but whatever would happen here on this planet will have a tremendous effect upon the other planets. The fallout of the atomic weapons would be carried to those planets creating a destruction and waste. Much of the fallout would go into space and hang there for centuries making interplanetary travel impossible. Death would be everywhere and birth almost impossible for new life would come into this world warped and strange looking.

All this must be prevented. The only way to stop it is to stop the nations from their hideous power plays. A religious revival will not be enough to stop all those ruthless, ambitious men from wanting to create a power struggle that will bring themselves on top for ruling. The use of fear instead of love must be stopped unless we desire to go down the drain, but this is actually withholding the long struggle of the Kali Yuga to finish and return eventually into another age of the golden era, after a long night of cosmic sleep for those who must stay.

The races have come and gone and those who are sharing the globe today are the sons and daughters of varied lands. Successive creation, slow elaborations of the earth at work, the continents emerging from the seas at great intervals of time, are what the ancient priests called the interdiluvian cycles. Within the ten races have actually been four colors, the red, yellow, black and white peoples. These have mainly been in existence since the world was engulfed by the great flood which sunk the Atlantis continent.

The red race of people is a descendent of the Atlantean races. They came down off the tops of the mountains, when their continent sank and the European land masses rose out of the seas, to higher grounds. They descended from the troglodytes, which were the red, or copper race on the continent of Atlantis. They were the primitive red race of the American Indians, and at this time settled in the southern part of Europe and eventually dominated the globe. They came to America over the land bridge between Siberia and Alaska, which is now the Bering Sea, in search of game and food. Game was plentiful until they almost wiped it out, and by the time the white man came to America the descendents of the original Indian race had left hardly anything but a few million of their race which had sunk back into an almost primitive stage.

Africa was the mother of the black race, called the Ethiopians by the Greeks. They built a large empire and a great civilization, which spread throughout the known world at that time and reached quite a height of culture. They invaded southern Europe and conquered the lands in which they made their military campaigns, but eventually were driven back by the white race. They have left a civilization which is found mainly in Abyssinia, East Africa and the Middle East.

The yellow race was that which came from Asia, and at one time the great people who had dominated the globe, but then retired back into China. It is in this country where the ancient civilization of the mother race of yellow people is still found.

The white race, or the Aryans sometimes called the Hyperboreans, came out of the northland and spread throughout the whole of Asia, India, Europe and some of Africa. These were the sandy-haired, blue-eyed men that came through the forests, illuminated by the aurora borealis, accompanied by dogs and reindeer, directed by bold leaders and clairvoyant women. They were shaggy haired, golden of skin and hair, and blue eyed. This race was to invent the worship of the sun and of the sacred fire, and would bring into the world a longing for heaven. Sometimes these people would have to rebel against heaven to the point of wanting to climb up to it, other times they would bow before its splendors in absolute adoration.

The white race, like the other races, had to tear itself away from the savage state before becoming aware of it. Its distinctive characteristics were the love of individual freedom, reflective sensitivity which creates the power of sympathy, and the supremacy of the intellect, which gives the imagination the idealistic and symbolic turn. This spiritual sensitivity brought about affection, man's preference for one wife, and his family, the conjugal principle. The need for freedom, coupled with that of sociability created the clan, and its elective principles of leadership and followers of an elected leader. Also visionary imagination created ancestor worship which formed the root and center of the religion of the white race.

In Asia, Iran and India, where people of the white race established the first Aryan civilization, mixing with the people of different colors, men quickly gained ascendancy over women in religious and political affairs. No longer did anyone speak except the wise men, and women had little to say except in the home. In Europe this was reversed and the women often took their place among the gods to help rule over the human race and women had equal rights in a great movement in both spiritual and material affairs among the northern race.

The white race fought the yellow, red and black races back and forth for many centuries from the Pyrenees to the Caucasus, and from the Caucasus to the Himalayas. The black race had settled in cities in the southern part of Europe, and their civilization old as it was included the most modern of military weapons in their day, armor of brass, iron weapons and good tactics. The half-savage whites had little more than stones, spears and bows and arrows. Defeated in the early part of their struggle to capture new lands, the white captives became the slaves of the blacks for labor in ore pits and stone quarries. Some escaped and came back with new ideas, skills and the science of their conquerors. Mainly they learned how to smelter metals and the recording of ideas by writing on the skins of animals or the bark of trees. These ideas have been passed down into modern civilization and created a part of our society today.

After the whites conquered the cities of the blacks in Europe and invaded the northern coasts of Africa they began to accept the ideas of certain parts of religions of the blacks. The idea of the oneness of the hidden, absolute and formless God was the essential core of the black religion, and its secret initiations.

All of what has been said here has had tremendous influence in the past and present, and will continue into the future. Because of the mixture between the two original religions: that of the white race which consists mostly of polytheism, and the black race which later developed into the Semitic peoples, with their idea of monotheism, two hostile streams of thought poured into the human race.

This is the basic problem today between the East and West. The Semitic and the Aryan currents are the two rivers of ideas upon which all our ideas, mythology, religion, art, science and philosophy have come to us. Each of these streams carries with itself a different conception of life, however the reconciliation and balance of the two would be truth itself, but the alienation of the two personalities of the leaders of every generation do not wish to bring together these two currents of thought.

The Semitic current contains what is said to be the idea of Absolute authority from a divine source, the idea of unity and universality in the name of a supreme principle which, in its application leads to the unification of the human family. This current represents the descending from God to man. The symbology is that of the punishing archangel who descends to earth, armed with sword and thunder.

The Aryan current contains the idea of ascending evolution in all terrestrial and supra-terrestrial kingdoms. Its application leads to an infinite diversity of developments in the richness of nature and the many aspirations of Soul. It is represented by Prometheus, who holds in his hand the fire snatched from heaven and surveys all heaven with a sweeping glance.

Every person carries these two currents within themselves. They think and act under the influence of one or the other in turn. But these currents are not harmoniously blended within ourselves. They contradict and fight one another in a struggle within our innermost feelings, in our subtle thoughts, as well as in our social life and institutions. What we could say here is that they respectively represent spirituality and naturalism, for they control our lives and our struggles while here on earth. The progress and salvation of mankind depends upon reconciliation and synthesis.

The conflicts of history have actually been wars of cults, when one delves deeply into these world aggressions. The play of power politics enters into these wars, of course, but it's only the results of the conflicting ideas of the two currents which, when one gets beyond the surface, he can see.

The Semitic stream goes back into the ancient history of Egypt of course, where it was originated from its mixture with the black race. The Aryan goes back into the ancient period when these white peoples were gathered about their fires in their northern long houses, chanting to their olden gods. But these traditions even take us back into primitive times when they both appeared to be united in harmony. But this was during the Golden Age which we know as the Satya Yuga.

Following the Golden Age of man it began to split and there was grief and strife versus confidence, strength and serenity which mankind has never recaptured. Now we begin to learn what is going to happen to mankind in the future while he is still an inhabitant of this earth world. Despite whatever people say who are apparently highly intelligent, these two streams are getting further apart. It is almost now the East versus the West, as if a wall has been drawn down over the countries dominated by China and Russia against any ideas entering into their countries or any of their ideas coming out except for propaganda. The same is true on the western side of the world.

Unless these two streams again become united, which apparently they do not seem to ever be, there will be the great blowup between the East and West. If ever anyone feels that he has witnessed destruction, or read of it in modern times, he knows nothing until the atomic blasts strike his cities.

Only blind wishful thinking will permit us to believe that our society is free from insidious influencing forces around us. These are exposed in the ECK-Vidya readings so many times so that each individual can learn what endangers him be it witchcraft, or some force which is going to use him as a victim for propaganda purposes. Constant pressures which he may be subjected to from the forces which are working upon him can be devised to break him down mentally. For example he can go through humiliation, rough inhuman treatment, degradation, intimidation, hunger, exposure to cold, all of which have been used and are being used on the masses today to crumble the will of the people and to soften them.

The fact is that such invisible and visible enemies of the two currents of thought working against one another, have brought each respectively under ruthless forces which are using these twin streams for their own purposes. They are matching them against one another in hopes of taking over the human race. This is the purpose of the totalitarian governments who want to rule the worlds, as well as the other planets. They know that the key to conquest doesn't lie in land armies occupying great masses of land, or ships that have control of the sea lanes. But it's that nation who has space platforms and bases on other planets, such as the moon so that they could threaten the whole earth globe with atomic weapons. The knowledge is whosoever controls the moon or other planets shall control the earth.

It is extremely difficult to escape the mechanically repeated suggestions of everyday life. Even when our critical mind rejects the negative inflow, they seduce us into doing what our intellect tells us is stupid. The mechanization of modern life has already influenced man to become more passive and to adjust himself to ready-made conformity. No longer does man think in personal values, following his own conscience and ethical evaluations, he thinks in the values brought him by mass media. Headlines in the morning newspapers give him his temporary political outlook, the radio blasts into his ears, the television keeps him in continual awe and passive fixation. He may consciously protest against these anonymous voices, but nevertheless their suggestions ooze into his mental system.

What is perhaps the most shocking about these insidious influences is that many of them have developed not out of man's destructiveness, but out of his hope to improve the world and to make his life richer and deeper. The very institutions man has created, the very progress he has made toward mastery of himself and his environment, all can become weapons of destruction.

The dangers do not lie in the fact that the atomic weapons are going to be explored and will destroy millions, but the very threat of this is hung over our heads by the governments of nations who are playing power politics. This awful propaganda alone makes man helpless. In no way can man defend himself against all this sort of danger, for it is in every thing around him, in all the mass media, in speeches, pamphlets, posters, billboards, radio and TV shows. What we call the will of the people, or the will of the masses, we only get to know after such collective action is put on the move, after the will of the people has been expressed either at the polls or in fury and rebellion. This indicates how important it is who is directing the tools and machines of public opinion.

This is why the ECK-Vidya is important, for it begins to tell those who are interested how to defend themselves against these terrible threats, which will break up the family unit, the community and the nation. A nation is composed only of people and therefore it depends upon the attitude and the will of the people to take over and manage it, to make it a good country in which to live.

All the things which have been said in this chapter can come about, however, they do not have to. So far we are heading in that direction and when we come to the end of the Kali Yuga, the age in which we are now living, it appears that most of the planet and others in this universe will be destroyed. This destruction will be on a cosmic level, and therefore will take in the lower planes which we call the psychic planes because this is God's will and we shall be taken care of, whether it be that we are consciously drawn up into the heavenly worlds, to sleep or be fully aware of what has taken place and join the company of the superior Souls there.

Anyone who has been following the path of ECK and comes into this era of destruction, will be saved by the Mahanta, the living ECK Master. However if there are enough channels for the ECK, that is if enough people can become channels under the direction of the Mahanta, the living ECK Master, in time perhaps we can keep this world intact a little longer, but this is the only way. These channels can prevent wars, and bring about a permanent peace provided there are enough of them developed by the Mahanta, the living ECK Master within the next few years. This is very important indeed for the survival of the human race.

CHAPTER 12

SOME CASE HISTORIES OF THE ECK-VIDYA READINGS

The science of the ECK-Vidya has been held in secrecy because very few people, when it was made public several centuries ago, cared to pay the seemingly high price that its exacting study demands. The ECK Masters withdrew it from the public because of this and other major factors responsible for the misunderstanding, among which a few have been the mystic and psychic characteristics attributed to this greatest of the prophetic sciences.

The most common misunderstanding was the discrediting of it by those who were in charge of the religious affairs in varied nations, the priestcraft and religious fanatics, to name a few along with those who felt the influence of the political power plays between the authorities of different countries, and between the rulers and peoples.

The history of ECKANKAR, the Ancient Science of Soul Travel, from which the ECK-Vidya springs, has gone underground in the past because of persecution from the orthodox religions of their own times. It submerged under Gopal Das, during the early Egyptian period about 3,000 years before the Christian era began. Those responsible for the submerging were the Nine Unknown ECK Masters, who are better known as the 'Council of the Nine,' in ECKANKAR.

They have purposely hidden ECKANKAR, and its 32 aspects, including the ECK-Vidya, from the eyes of the mundane masses because of the vicious attacks being made upon It. In other words they have felt that it's better to work in almost silence with a few than have to be in the eyes of the public and defend ECK, maybe with force, in the same manner that many of the orthodox religions have had to do in the past and present.

The common misinterpretations have been due in part to the

179

reluctance of the true and authoritative adepts of the Ancient Order of the Vairagi to divulge the inner secrets and mysteries of the ultimate knowledge of ECK to inquisitive laymen, curious scholars and uninitiated philosophers. Those who are not prepared to enter the field and explore the glorious realm of the spiritual heavens through a prescribed disciplined system of living, essential for advancement in the study and spiritual experiments of ECK, are not worthy of admission into the sanctuary of ECKANKAR.

This is one of the main reasons why few ECK Masters will ever give an ECK-Vidya reading outside his own followers. They know the general public follower of these arts is not capable of understanding what he has said in the reading. This is somewhat true of some of those who actually follow him because he goes into such depth and has such a broad and deep interpretation on the readee's life that sometimes the points are completely missed. It means then that the ECK Master has to go back over again and try to explain what has taken place.

The ECK Masters realize that many people cannot accept the findings of the ECK-Vidya, therefore they would not be able to bring it out as a mass item, certainly not like Astrology with all its popularity, not like an akashic reading which has to deal with past lives; not even like a Soul reading which is that of the incarnations of Soul between the upper planes. Sometimes the broadness and the depth of an ECK-Vidya reading is too much for the client and because of his misunderstanding, it only works against the ECK-Vidya reader.

Another factor for this lack of understanding about the ECK-Vidya has been the superficial and incompetent reports and interpretations of the ECK-Vidya brought and talked about by some western travelers who had been fortunate to visit India and Tibet over the centuries. On the other hand we owe a great deal to some of the ECK Masters like Fubbi Quantz and Rebazar Tarzs who have introduced the light of ECKANKAR to the world on a universal scale.

Europe has not been without its secret ECK Masters and hidden ECK centers under various names during the millenniums. The Hermetics, Pythagorian and Platonic philosophers, the Stoics, and others practiced ECK under different names and interpretations to fit their particular systems of thought. Some of the elect leaders of the secret circles and orders had continuous contact with the adepts of the Vairagi in the Himalayan centers of light and wisdom, who were in the remote country of Tibet.

Some of the readings which the ECK-Vidya give are part of the training and background that the ECK chela must get before he is able to understand his own nature. One of the better type of readings is given here so that you might have a grasp on what is being said. It is taken in part or parts and the name of the individual is not given.

"You have a very deep problem which must be overcome in this lifetime. This problem consists of introvertism, or that of being so cautious and reserved in nature that it is holding you back. In fact it did not come within a single lifetime, but is a holdover from a time when you were a young man in the fifteenth century and were arrested in Italy for being reported for having said certain things against the church. The traumatic experience and shock which you underwent certainly left its mark so that it has been several lifetimes getting to that point whereby it can be erased forever. Meanwhile it has a deeper meaning for you; all this timidity, reserve with people and the conservative way that you feel about life is that underlying fear. These various points just named here are the outer manifestations of this underlying fear.

"Actually this fear created back in the fifteenth century, and which I won't get into the circumstances too much, has brought a deep traumatic scar which has been with you for a long time. It has influenced your life so long that it has become something which you have lived with all these different lives, and it also brought you to the Mahanta, the living ECK Master, so that you may find the freedom from it. This shall be done, for you now have found the right source in which you will get the freedom from this fear."

This was only a section taken out of an ECK-Vidya reading. Although you might believe that it is necessary to have the whole of a single reading, it is best not to get into the larger sections of an ECK-Vidya reading until later. However, this man since his reading learned how to take control of this fear, by practicing certain specific exercises which have been given him. He now leads a normal life, has since been married, has two healthy children and looks as if he is going to the top of his country in leadership.

Now all ECK-Vidya readings will give this type of inner problems; some will be about the future of the individual, just like some of the regular readings, while others may take up another aspect of the individual's life. It is what the ECK-Vidya reader sees is necessary to tell the readee. If he has to dig into past lives this will be done; but it's not always true of him doing so. Nobody gets the same type reading, which can almost be said of an akashic reading. There is always a sameness in the akashic readings, mainly for the reason that when tracing a person's past lives down through the centuries it appears that most people outwardly lived about the same type of experiences, that is in the external worlds. Now their experiences are practically the same in the outer worlds, but not the inner, and sometimes it might even appear that two or more persons were the same individual. In some cases two of them might have been practically twins and lived the same type of life. This has even thrown me at times trying to find out just what these people were doing in some past lives which make them look the same. Having traced out two or more in this sort of thing it gets a little embarrassing to try to put these readings together and yet make them appear different. But I am not the only one who has been put in this position, for several very good readers in other fields have told me the same thing.

Another type of ECK-Vidya reading has gone something like this in parts:

"In taking a look at your life, that is the future, I want to warn you of what might happen in the month of June this year. You already have quite a large portfolio of blue ribbon stocks. I would particularly watch certain stocks like the airline industry which appears to be on a downward swing starting in the month of June. You should have a long talk with your broker about this and start selling out fast, provided it doesn't stop before the end of June. This is one way of helping yourself if at all possible, and it will bring a lot more comfort of mind and peace if you are watchful of your own properties at this particular period of the year."

It is seldom that an ECK-Vidya reader will give information in a reading like this. He usually steers away from some material data which might mislead the client who would take his words outwardly and act upon them without thought. Like all other readings the client must study the reading just like he would study any report which he must do.

These readings are interesting from the standpoint that they will fit the client and not any person. Since it's the duty of the Mahanta, the living ECK Master, to take care of all his chelas in this world who have been gathered to him, he will say things to them which certainly has little meaning at the time that he speaks. But the individual must wait and ponder what has been said in order to find out what the data means and where it can be used, or where it is applied in his life.

The one noticeable thing which an ECK Master will do is to never give the client or chela more than he can accept at that particular time in mind or body. He knows the acceptance level of every individual who is under his guidance and protection. He knows that every person who is following him has a certain level of awareness and learning ability. If he is to be stretched out just a little further it must be done gradually and not all at once. Certain persons who step onto the path of ECK for the first time will run into problems, no matter what their background has been in metaphysics or religious training. They are not prepared for what is to come for them when the Mahanta, the living ECK Master, starts breaking down all the teachings and instructions which have been ground into them by other lines of religious and spiritual works. He must rapidly refill these holes which he has pulled out of the chela with something within ECK, and if the chela cannot accept it, he must suffer in the sense of instability for awhile until he can accept what is being done here on the level of acceptance by the mental processes of the client.

Another reading went something like this:

"You have asked something about Soul mates. I would advise you not to approach a marriage in this manner, but put it in a more practical ground. Of course there will always be a chemistry of the inner nature between two people which may mislead you that this is your Soul mate.

"Since you have spent a considerable amount of time looking for someone whom you believe is a Soul mate for you, and this hasn't happened until recently when a man approached you with the same idea, and now you want to know, even after a bad experience with him. My answer is that this man is not for you.

"However, I do tell you that on the 9th of June this year you will meet a man from Boston, who is tall, well built and gentle in manner. This conduct is natural and very good and will fit your personality well. He will within two months ask you to marry him, and if you still feel the same way do so for he is the best that you can find at this particular time. And since he has money of his own he will not be interested in your financial status.

"The one thing which you must remember is that life is going to be a bumpy road regardless. Not even those who go out into isolation, away from all peoples, have an easy time of it. When two people join in marriage at your ages they always have a certain amount of adjusting to do which is harder than marrying when young. Marriage is also a bumpy road because two people have a harder time communicating with one another as they grow older, no matter how close they may be in companionship."

This reading was mainly concerned with a woman who had put off several opportunities to be married because she felt that her true Soul mate had not shown up yet. Of course this is a carry-over from another life, in fact a series of lives, but she was making a very serious mistake. The mistake wasn't that she hadn't found the right man to suit her, which she hadn't of course, but her premise was wrong. She was mixing social obligations with spiritual matters.

Marriage is really a social obligation to reproduce children, but it is also an emotional fulfillment for both a man and woman. Since this woman was over fifty her opportunities for marriage were growing less every year. It wasn't going to be long before she would be out of that area where few if any males would be interested in her except for her money, and to marry anyone for their money alone is a terrible burden for both parties involved.

There is also the problem of being mixed in the emotions about people who are ready for marriage and can't quite make the step. The woman always feels that it's a greater step to take than the man because she is going to lose her identity and be dependent upon somebody that she really doesn't know anyway. There again if she is trying marriage to reform the man in question from some vice, she is only wasting her time. Some men can be reformed but the majority cannot for they are always interested in their own vices more than people, especially wives who are trying to get them to stop whatever it is they are doing wrong whether it's alcoholism or gambling.

Soul mates have already been explained in another chapter so we won't go into this except to see that the emotional patterns of two people, man and woman, sometimes fit together well so the problems between them over the years will not be too much.

We now enter into another type of problem which has come up time and again with those who are trying to follow the spiritual path of ECK and seemingly cannot see nor understand that they have made any spiritual progress whatsoever. This is always a sad case indeed because of the problem which is so hidden that few people can see it whatsoever.

Generally a person is introverted and cannot see anything objectively. He thinks in terms of subjectivism and this is not good because the whole purpose of life is to be able to take a good look at one's self both objectively and subjectively. In other words be in control of one's self, that is his own viewpoint and not to react to negative things. He should be the actor and not the reactor.

Part of the problem which we are concerned with went something like this:

"I keep wondering just what is wrong here. I do not seem to make any spiritual progress whatsoever. I stay depressed and unhappy and nothing seems to come out just right. As a matter of fact I don't even feel like doing my spiritual exercises of ECKAN-KAR. Whenever I try the spiritual exercises, I simply seem to do nothing but sit there with my mind going around in a whirl. Can't think of anything but how much I am failing to do things right.

"Is there something which can be done for me? Does it look as if I can ever do anything with my spiritual development? Where am I now on the path to God? I need help badly and think you are just the one to help me, and this is the reason why I am writing you for an ECK-Vidya reading."

The answer that went into part of the reading went like this:

"Few people have ever existed who did not have depressions, the miseries and general unhappiness. Not even the holy men, nor the saints ever existed in which they did not believe that God had deserted them. Take a look at the story of Job. I do not expect there has ever been a time when a person went through the same thing as Job did in his exile from God.

"This is what is generally known as the dark night of Soul. I speak about this in length in the first series of tapes which were done on ECK called the Purpose of ECKANKAR. One believes that God has deserted him but this isn't true, for that person who has hit these depths is only going through a part of his karma where he is just passing off such a load that it seems impossible for him to ever carry on again. This is something like the old axiom 'darkness before dawn.'

"You will be in this state for a period of three months: July, August and September. Then you will start coming out of it about

185

the first of October and proceed up the ladder with your spiritual unfoldment. It's like passing from night into dawn and thereby gaining the light of day to see all that could not be seen in the darkness. But this I promise you that when you have come out of this darkness and have been lifted up to a higher plane, that never again will you have to go through the same amount of karma as you did in the past.

"Be patient because three months is little time in your whole life in eternity. It is yourself who is responsible and by acting in faith you can bring about new happiness and love for yourself and those who are nearest and dearest to you. If the saints can do this, if those who have not even been saints, or holy in their nature can go through the dark night of Soul, so can you. It will be hard but put your faith in the Mahanta, the living ECK Master and all will be well."

In this reading I had to go back into several lives, as many as two hundred for this woman, researching, checking and trying to work out the real reason for this woman's troubles at the present time. Naturally she had run into the problem of getting stuck on the level of the dark night of Soul, but at the same time she had to see the problem on a practical level. She had to know and at the same time feel what was going on within herself. She would have never been satisfied with a single explanation of anything.

These cycles of deep depressions usually roll in on a person about every three years, sometimes six to nine, and last for a considerable time; often the same length of time as the cycle, for example if it's three years, it would last a year and a half; or if it was six years it might last three years, and again it might last for the full period of six years before going out again. In order to learn what is the natural cycle of the individual I had to do the research on her past lives in order to judge whether this was another cycle which sometimes comes with the individual in his natural life, or whether it was one which she had hit in her spiritual unfoldment.

Naturally it was the period in which she had for spiritual unfoldment. She did come out of it later with a beautiful insight on what had happened and frankly a much happier person and certainly her ability to meet with the problems of life had improved considerably.

There are many other types of problems which come up in the ECK-Vidya readings, which are most important to the clients but we can say that they usually fall in the following category: (1) Spiritual Matters, (2) Money, (3) Health, and (4) Family. Generally they fall in this order and the ECK Master giving the reading must consider which he believes to be the first in the category which will be resolved for the readee.

Other things of importance to the clients are often: How to gain psychic control over others, how to get one's wife or husband to return, and how to gain psychic powers so that one can become rich, healthy and famous. And of course we don't want to forget that many people want to know what their past lives have been; they mainly want to know this because it's like a family tree which gives a non-social status person, a social standing. Many people make claims to being someone famous in the past in either the religious field or the historical affairs of mankind. If a reader or clairvoyant tells a woman that she has been Cleopatra in a past life this person might try to use it as a social background. I have seen many a person make claims of being the Mother Mary, and in this life tell others about this with all the sincerity and honesty they could muster.

These people are not being dishonest in their own thinking and neither are they harming anyone in society by doing this. So I have always felt that nothing should be done about them because this might give them an ego boost whereby nothing else does. As I say, as long as they are not doing any particular harm to others either mentally or physically we should overlook this.

However, the ECK Masters try to give a readee nothing but the straight answers, and if a person served out a number of lives in very humble positions, they should be told and the reasons why that he has been an individual low on the social pole of life.

The secret of reading an individual is to teach him not to look backwards, but to look ahead. This is one of the main problems of every individual, he wants to know where he has been and not where he is going in life. Death generally comes when spiritual decay prepares its way; spiritual decay sets in when the mind ceases its growth, loses its interest in the future, and withdraws its attention from the world and all its knowledge and its fascinating beauties. When the self relinquishes its faculties and repudiates its wonderful power through ignorance, the disintegration of the forces that hold the body together will start, then slowly but surely the end of it draws near.

This is why the individual should not be so interested in past life readings but in future life readings. Since he is a part of that which we call eternity he should then accept all that has been his life in the past and that is going to be his life in the future as a whole. Quickly as he accepts this attitude then all life begins to fall into place. Truth is a part of him and the one way of getting truth is through the ECK-Vidya, which can give him all his past lives, all his present life and all his future lives. When he gets these all fitted together then the whole of his life is complete.

The problem here is that when man is seeking out and if he is able to accept all of life via the human senses then he is able to know all things, but it's hardly possible. Because his senses will not allow him to encompass all life, he is forever searching. He doesn't know that the only way to grasp the whole of life is through his spiritual senses.

One of the worst concepts of our modern times is brought over from the Oriental belief that man should spend a considerable amount of time in introspective thought. That he should sit in contemplation for hours looking deeply within himself to resolve all his problems. This doesn't happen to be true; this is the worst of all the practices that he could use for spiritual advancement.

This is why the ECK-Vidya became such a force in man's life. It tries to pull the individual away from this introspective idea; not that it doesn't believe in it, but when anyone tries to look inwardly at himself and his faults he is going to have troubles. This is particularly true when he spends long periods of time in introspection.

The ECK-Vidya wants its own clients to spend a modest amount of time in contemplation for when one overdoes this he runs into both mental and physical health problems. For example a reading for one in the ECK-Vidya went like this:

"Your health problem is basically that you are spending too much time alone in contemplation, and in the lotus position. You are first a westerner and not used to spending much time alone, because you have a certain amount of inborn social duties to do like being with people and communicating with people; this comes out of your childhood, especially true of yourself. You cannot do things which are contrary to your nature. This is one of the main reasons for you being upset most of the time; you are growing too sensitive to life and no matter what happens you are really trying to hide instead of advance spirtually in Soul growth.

"Secondly, the problems with your knees and ankles which you spoke about is that you are sitting too long in a position which involves your circulation and joints of your lower extremities. In time this will weaken your legs which should be the strongest part of you, for when you get any age and have circulatory problems believe me it's a great handicap.

"You might say, well it doesn't seem to harm the holy man who is able to sit in a lotus position for long periods of time, year after year. Nor does it seem to hurt the Buddhists who do the same type of practice. This isn't altogether true, for it's very apparent that the Orientals who do practice such positions in their religious rites have a weakness of legs, and lower body. It also is apparent that the position does cramp the lower intestines and creates a stomach and lower bowel disorder in many cases. Not all, but in lots of cases.

"You may feel as some people do that the lotus position and that which is close to this position, what we call the tailor fashion or semi-lotus way of contemplation, brings one into great enlightenment and this alone brings the body great health. Because it does give such health benefits then it's good for all the body and it doesn't hurt the legs, and other parts of the body.

"Naturally there hasn't been any statistics about the statements I am making on this but one of the things which is found and not talked about is that the lotus, yoga or any type position of this nature does bring about certain health problems and no matter how much enlightenment, or contact with God, it isn't going to help you. The health conditions of the psychic conditions of man especially in yoga is often temporary, and it's only the exercises which are of benefit to man, not the positions. So think this over please for it could be one of the problems which you are having at this time and which could be cleared up by sitting in a straight chair with your feet flat on the floor, back straight, chin up, while in your periods of contemplation."

This is actually working in the metaphysical field and it won't put itself together with the ECK-Vidya, nor will it put itself together for religious functions. Too many people mix the two and have little results and certainly wonder why.

Actually the very reason that metaphysics and religion will not function properly together is because metaphysics represents power and religion love. The two do not come together as a single stream but must co-exist side by side, just as love and hate must do the same. If one neglects the other he is bound to have some sort of troubles.

The ECK-Vidya therefore must work through all the planes, including the solid material planes, the psychic planes and the spiritual planes. It does not stop with one area like metaphysics or religions do. It works in the over-all field of the individual, never one-sided so that the vibrations are cut off in one area, and let go full blast in another area of consciousness within the individual being read.

The ECK-Vidya is working basically with the sound current, therefore it works with the idea or stages of transformation, scanning the ethereal, invisible, and audible realms for anything which might be abberations in the readee, regardless of what plane it might be on. But it is mainly concerned with the full range and breadth of the individual's being, and not just a part of him as the other mantic sciences might be.

Words stir thought on the mental level, inspiration or feeling on the astral level and intuition on the spiritual level. When we think about speech being sacred, and as a combination of atoms, combined by the force of certain notes, sounds or vibrations, we start a discipline of our speech to keep it from being destructive or be more constructive. Speech provides in its constructive role the particular note to hurl atoms of energy into activity and production of forms, and in its destructive role becomes the factor of disintegration of the atoms of form.

This is the secret of the creative power of speech. Its attracting potency transforms it into a huge magnet that draws to itself with immense impact the concrete image of its original purpose. So we find that we must take extreme care which is indispensable in the selection of words and utterance of speech, for each word is a powerful magnet attracting or producing what it calls for or represents.

Speech or the words of man is a combination of coherent sounds; and sounds by themselves, regardless of their different meanings in different languages, have certain inherent potencies as we have just given here. These potencies are by nature either beneficial or maleficent according to their positive or negative vibration, wave-length and rate of frequency. This is why certain words, or names, produce a pleasant reaction regardless of their meanings, and others produce an annoying reaction and an unpleasant effect regardless of their meanings.

The Mahanta, the living ECK Master, must at all times try to present a positive form of speech. Because he must deal with people on various levels of consciousness, this is understanding, he is always conscious of what he must say in public. Not all people will understand what he is saying during a public talk, because they are not trained in the way of the ECK. They are trained in the way of the Kal, the negative.

The Mahanta, the living ECK Master, is also a realist. He knows how to use the ECK and the Kal in this world. We live in this material plane, or in what is better known to the ECKists as a Kal world. There is no such thing as a totally ECK, or positive person, and vice versa, and since we live in a world of matter and Kal influence we have all got to contain a certain amount of negativism within us to merely keep alive and to adapt to the needs of this materialistic world.

The whole problem lies here in the fundamental principle that long as we are living within this world of matter we are trained to be negative from birth, to be at least materialists enough to learn to support ourselves. We are in other words trained to react to manifestation of any sort. We are schooled to become the slaves of phenomena. Since the negative is decay and death, we are schooled less in the art of living than in the art of dying. And this is what the ECK-Vidya is all about, it trains its own to be positive about the act of death.

The Mahanta is trying to tell you through the ECK-Vidya that to become independent of the things of this world, is to simply don't need it, and let the world see that you don't need it. This packs a thousand percent more wallop than anything which you might do in this world. Of course you will be running into a problem here because few people ever want anyone else to become freedmen. You are surrounded by a mass of negativism and you had best use your judgment as to when you show your freedom for the majority of the human race has been trained to be Kalistic (negative), and are not able to bring themselves to believe that there is anything like a real person who might be free of any of the works of the negative.

This is where the ECK-Vidya enters into the understanding for anyone who has asked for such a reading. It represents the positive aspects in anyone's life who wants to know the truth about

191

himself whether it be that of the smallest thing in his life, to that of the highest. It runs the whole gamut of the individual's life from the act of some daily minor deed to the major act of spiritual unfoldment. Nothing is too small about anyone to catch the eye and attention of the ECK-Vidya reader. All must be taken into consideration in order to make up the full reading whether or not the reader tells him.

We attain the spiritual ultimate in ECK when we have earned it, and not before, and since greed, hatred and wars on every side prove that we have not mastered this material plane yet, it's best to set our own individual affairs in order before worrying about the next world. Too many people want to work for the next world, but since they are going to get there without any urgency on anyone else's part it's best to be a little patient about what life is over there. It's best to pay attention to what we are doing here instead, in order to make it right when we get there.

The matter of mind control must be taken in consideration here. There are some today who believe that everything can be controlled by the mind which is certainly impossible. One believes that certain formulas which can be repeated may bring them success with healing, money, love and health. There are a number of books today on the market on mind control connected with being a dazzling success with and through the mind. These are mostly how to make the subconscious do what one wants and some sort of success in particular fields without training or preparation. This simply isn't true because we must pay for everything that we get in life, and no amount of control of the mind is going to change us from ignorance to success in the classroom, or in industry without preparing ourselves some way to get to that point of success needed. The whole problem here is that too many people believe that the mind can be controlled.

The mind is either a great task master, or a great slave. The only control that anyone can have over his mind is to take it out of the grooves in which it has established itself. It is a creature of habit and doesn't have much to offer anybody except to be a disturber of that individual's peace, or to allow it to have peace.

One trains the mind in the same sense that it would train a dog or a child. It must learn certain habits which can be established by certain formulas, but must be carried on for years in order to take hold and allow the individual to become master over himself. But at the same time he is also dealing with emotions which bring to him fear, grief and anger. These are to be taken into consideration when one is trying to get control of himself.

What those don't understand is that when one is talking about mind control he means the psychic energy. This is the universal mind stuff, or the negative power that they are talking about. When one begins to deal with this power to make himself wealthy, famous, and healthy it is merely manipulating the power itself. But the catch here is that sooner or later the action or deed has run its course and the individual who is using manipulation will come to a stop for the psychic power is like the flow of a tide, it comes and goes in waves and the person trying it suddenly finds out that his power has left. He becomes terribly frustrated, and the effect of his own effect. Nobody can help him at this particular point except the Mahanta, the living ECK Master, and it's doubtful whether it would be done at this point either by him. For the ECK Master usually allows everybody to work out their own karmic patterns of life without getting into the act itself. All this is, one finds upon examination, is that he has not gained anything regardless of what the outer worldly appearances might be in his case, except more karma to work off. This is also true in everything one does which is concerned with the psychic power.

The ECK-Vidya is the true way of learning about yourself, for the past, present and future. In fact it is the one way!

INDEX

Eshwar-Khanwale (God Eaters), 118
Eternal Light and Sound, 138
Etheric
    Aura, 107
    Body, 59
    Plane, 11, 12, 18, 33, 51, 52, 53, 70, 121, 126, 137, 168
    World, 119
Europe, 156, 170, 180
European Countries, 156
Eye
    All-seeing, 152
    Evil, 152
    Nukti-i-saveda, 152
    of Shiva, 152
    Shiva-Netra, 152
    Sightless, 152
    Spiritual, 152
    Third, 152
    Tisra Til, 152
Facets of spiritual works, 7
False Prophets, 117
Far East, 154
Farank (Year of Full Moon), 31, 53, 88, 90, 95
Fate Karma (Praabdh), 45
Feminine Principle, 154
Future Karma (Sinchit), 45
Fifth
    Circle Initiate, 23, 38, 39
    Loses Karma via Mahanta, 67
    Plane, 15, 28, 33, 51, 87, 152
    Ruler of Plane, 58
Field of magnetism, 15
Field of total awareness, 12
Five
    foolish virgins, 151
    -pointed star, 150
    wise virgins, 151
Fountains of knowledge, 117

218

Soul

BOOK ORDER COUPON

Mail to:

ECKANKAR
P.O. Box 3100
Menlo Park, California 94025 U.S.A.

☐ Please send me a free book catalog.

I enclose $＿＿＿ for the book(s) checked below.

International Orders: Please remit Int'l Money Order or check payable in U.S. funds to ECKANKAR.

QTY

＿＿＿ 0104 **In My Soul I Am Free** $2.95

＿＿＿ 0106 **The Tiger's Fang** $2.50 papbk

＿＿＿ 010699 **The Tiger's Fang** $8.95 hb

＿＿＿ 0110 **Your Right to Know** $1.95 papbk

＿＿＿ 011099 **Your Right to Know** $8.95 hb

＿＿＿ 011299 **From Heaven to the Prairie** $14.95 hb

＿＿＿ 0126 **The Flute of God** $2.95

＿＿＿ 0128 **The Spiritual Notebook** $2.95

＿＿＿ 0132 **Stranger by the River** $5.95

＿＿＿ 0154 **Letters to Gail, Vol. I** $5.95 papbk

＿＿＿ 0155 **Letters to Gail, Vol. II** $9.95 hb

＿＿＿ 0188 **The Wind of Change** $3.95 papbk

＿＿＿ 018899 **The Wind of Change** $6.95 hb

Total $＿＿＿

6% sales tax (California only) $＿＿＿

Add 10% for shipping $＿＿＿
75¢ minimum

TOTAL ENCLOSED $＿＿＿

Name ＿＿＿＿＿＿＿＿＿＿＿＿＿＿＿＿＿
(please print)

Street ＿＿＿＿＿＿＿＿＿＿＿＿＿＿＿＿＿

City＿＿＿＿＿＿＿＿＿＿＿ State＿＿＿＿

Country ＿＿＿＿＿＿＿＿ Postal Code＿＿＿

(detach here)

194

(detach here)

☐ Please send me more information on ECKANKAR.

☐ I am interested in information on discussion or study groups in my area.

Mail to:

ECKANKAR
P.O. Box 3100
Menlo Park, California 94025
U.S.A.

Name _____
       (please print)

Street _____

City _____ State_____

Country _____ Postal Code_____